D1257023

Industry in Action

Young Workers

D. N. Ashton
Lecturer in the Department of Sociology, University of Leicester
and
David Field
Lecturer in the Department of Sociology, University of Leicester

Hutchinson of London

Hutchinson & Co (Publishers) Ltd
3 Fitzroy Square, London W1

London Melbourne Sydney Auckland
Wellington Johannesburg and agencies
throughout the world

First published in 1976
© D. N. Ashton and David Field 1976

Set in Monotype Baskerville
Printed in Great Britain by The Anchor Press Ltd
and bound by Wm Brendon & Son Ltd
both of Tiptree, Essex

ISBN 0 09 127370 6

Contents

Contents

Acknowledgements

We wish to thank Gill Ashton for her general support, help and encouragement. We also thank Professor Alexander for his helpful suggestions.

This book originates from Ashton's work with Norbert Elias. While acknowledging this very real debt we do not wish to imply that Professor Elias would agree with the ideas we express and the interpretations we have made.

We thank the secretarial staff of our department for their help. In particular we thank Mo Thompson for her skill (and patience) in transforming our untidy and somewhat illegible drafts into fair copy, and Doreen Butler for typing the final draft in its entirety.

There are a large number of other people whom it is impossible to thank individually who contributed in various ways to the making of this book. These include young workers themselves, teachers, youth workers, careers officers, and academic colleagues. We thank them all.

DAVID FIELD
D. N. ASHTON

May 1976

Editorial Foreword

A combination of factors makes it difficult for the practising manager or trade unionist to form a broad and forward view of modern industrial society and his or her role within it. Pressures of work and living, narrowing specializations, the increasing role of external influences particularly from government, and the pace and diversity of change all conspire against such understanding. The expanding demands of specialized functions have affected education and intellectual activity generally, compartmentalizing thought and knowledge and in particular tending to exclude social issues and values and to isolate industrial theory and practice from society in a dangerously unreal way.

Despite welcome developments in both the quantity and quality of education for industry, perspectives are still blocked by the preconceptions of yesterday and the preoccupations of today. Even the younger manager attending a course has to make a considerable effort first to widen his view and then to integrate all that comes within it. The books in this series *Industry in Action* are designed to complement the individual efforts of those managers, trade unionists, students and others who wish to take this wider view. Within the framework set by the need to understand the complex forces which are re-shaping industry and society each book will impart the specialist knowledge and techniques relevant to its area of interest and seek to establish and explore the links between the specialism and technological, social, political and other influences which are relevant to them.

The problems of young workers can be treated both at the individual and the social levels, and this book covers both. Partly because empirical work drawn upon by the authors challenges the generally held view that the transition from school to work is a period of strain, tension and even trauma for a majority of young people, the authors place considerable emphasis upon the social and industrial implications of the experiences of young people in modern industrial society. Their analysis reaches back in time to the influence of family and school and forward to the attitudes to work established as the young person moves through adolescence to maturity, and because of this there is much in the book which will be of interest to educationists and social workers as well as to managers and in particular to personnel managers.

A feature of the book is that a number of previously distinct branches of knowledge are brought to bear on its subject and it backs this up with recommendations for further reading drawn from several disciplines and approaches.

There is very little encouragement for those who expect some combination of legislation and a re-structuring of authority and decision-taking in industry to yield quick benefits in the form of changed attitudes and behaviour from productive workers. Educational and family influences may prove long lasting and more powerful than any new initiatives taken at the place of work, and even when hopeful changes are instituted in education as well as in industry, it will take a long time for these changes to permeate and produce new attitudes on a substantial scale. Such realism about the time scale of social change is not taken as a reason for inertia, however, but leads the authors to advocate that an early start be made to reforms in each of the relevant sectors. A virtue of the book is the clear way in which the earlier sections on the contemporary situations of young workers are related to the policies proposed.

The four individual case studies at the end of the book provide valuable illustrative material and readers may find it useful to read them along with chapters 3, 4 and 5. Although a major finding and theme of the book is the considerable extent to which the employment histories of individuals are influenced, even pre-determined, by family and education, the authors do provide a valuable treatment of the problem of upward and downward social mobility.

K.J.W.A.

1. Introduction

In this book our concern is to understand the behaviour of certain types of young people and their problems of adjustment to work. In the academic literature we could find very little which dealt with the experiences of these young people in a unitary way. Rather, their different areas of activity were treated in isolation, and as if they bore no relation to other areas of young people's lives. The sociology of the family, the sociology of education, and industrial sociology each contributed to our understanding of the young people and their problems, but only within the confines of their own specialist areas and in terms of their own particular concerns, and often without reference to developments in social psychology. It was in this context that one of us with a background in industrial sociology (the senior author, Ashton) and the other with a background in social psychology (Field) came together in an attempt to examine in a systematic and unitary manner the experiences the young people had in the different areas of their lives.

When reviewing the literature in the fields just mentioned, and in analysing interviews of young people who had only been in work for a few years,[1] our attention was drawn to three considerations. The first of these was that contrary to a fairly widely accepted belief expressed in the literature, most young people did *not* experience severe problems of adjustment in the course of their transition from school to work. It is widely accepted by academics and others more directly involved with youth that the period of transition from school to work is stressful for the young people concerned. Such a view appears to be grounded in 'common sense', in that these young people are isolated from the world of work in separate educational institutions and then suddenly released on to the labour market. It thus appears to make sense to argue that they are likely to experience a form of shock on their exposure to the world of work. However, as the results of more empirically based studies have come to light[2] it has become clear that most young people do *not* experience the transition from school to work as a period of particular stress or as involving them in traumatic problems of adjustment to their new position in the adult community. Rather, it appears that the previous experience of the young people in their home, school and peer group prepares them well to fit in or adjust to the demands imposed upon them on starting work.

The second consideration was the inability of the existing body of knowledge to account for the eagerness and obvious pleasure with which some young people enter what are often referred to as 'dead-end' jobs, and which most young people avoid.

A third consideration was how to explain the finding that in each of the occupational categories which we examined there was a small but significant number of young people who, although they appeared to have the same 'objective' characteristics as others in the category, obviously found their early years at work a frustrating and bitter experience. It was our attempt to explain the adjustment problems of this last group which led to the development of the ideas expressed in this book.

On closer examination of the evidence a distinct pattern began to emerge. It became clear that for most young people there is a basic continuity in their experience at home, at school, and at work, such that the kinds of beliefs they acquire about themselves and the perspectives they develop about the world at home and in the school are continually verified in their experience of work. This, we think, explains why it is that most young people do not experience severe problems of adjustment to work and why some of them may be happy to enter 'dead-end' jobs. It also explains why a small minority do experience severe problems of adjustment due to the discontinuity between the expectations and experiences transmitted and acquired at home and school and those encountered at work. What we shall argue in this book is that it

12

is crucial to any adequate understanding of the problems raised above to be aware of the 'subjective' experiences of young people. That is, we must try to understand the ways in which they experience the relationships they are a part of in the home, at school, and at work, and to do this without imposing prior images and ideas of the nature of the individual or of work upon such experiences.

DEFINITION OF TERMS

Perspectives

Before we proceed with our examination of the experiences and perspectives of young people we must clarify what is meant when we talk about *perspective* and *adjustment to work*. We use the term perspective to refer to the habitual ways of viewing themselves and the world which people hold. These perspectives provide a consistent way of viewing and interpreting the world which highlight some aspects of it at the expense of others. They develop out of everyday experiences, and once acquired are an important element in making sense of such experiences and in guiding behaviour. People located in different positions in our society have different experiences of work and different family and community relationships as a result of which they develop different perspectives. The perspectives are initially acquired in the family and for most people are reinforced by their experiences in later life.

The ideas that people have of their abilities, the requirements they have of work and the meanings they give to their work and leisure differ from one group to another. For example, human beings tend to establish certain boundaries within which they habitually think and act in relation to the work situations they face. It is already well established that those people who follow middle-class careers (e.g. teachers, managers and lawyers) tend to regard work as a central area of achievement. They tend to evaluate their own worth in terms of their success in their career and so give their other interests a more subordinate position in their scale of values. By contrast, many semi-skilled and unskilled workers tend to regard work merely as a necessary activity which they have to perform in order to provide the resources which enable them to pursue more worthwhile and interesting activities in their non-work hours. For this type of worker, work *cannot* serve as a significant sphere of achievement. In both groups these perspectives are reinforced partly by the 'objective nature' of the work situation and partly by the individual's interactions with others who hold the same perspective.

Adjustment to Work

The fact that different groups within the society tend to see themselves and the world of work in different ways has a number of important implications for any discussion of the problems of adjustment to work. The term *adjustment* when used with reference to human behaviour refers to the way in which people tend to change or modify their ideas, attitudes and behaviour in accordance with the demands or constraints of the situations they enter. In this sense our everyday life involves us in a continuous process of adjustment as we constantly shape, modify and adapt our ideas, attitudes and behaviour in the course of our interaction with others. These adaptations and modifications are not random, for they tend to take place within fairly clearly defined social boundaries. Also, the images we hold of ourselves – which in turn are created, maintained and transformed in the process of everyday interaction – play an important part in establishing the nature and extent of the adjustments we can and do make in our behaviour.

An initial distinction must be made between those adjustments which are made within the context of the perspectives which people hold and those which challenge or undermine them. The distinction may be clarified by looking at some examples of the everyday adjustments that young workers have to make during their first few years at work. Many of them find the working hours difficult to get used to after school, others find the behaviour of some adult workers difficult to get used to, and yet others find the 'bad' language of the adults difficult to adjust to. Another area of concern for some are problems of technique encountered in mastering their occupational skills. Yet none of these problems requires a fundamental change in the young persons' perspective either in terms of their abilities, or their orientation to work. Those who find the hours of work difficult to adjust to may have to change their sleeping habits. Similarly those who encounter problems in the acquisition of their occupational skills are usually able to surmount them with the help of college courses, correspondence courses or with the help of the older workers.

While it is important that we are aware of these adjustment problems, the point to be stressed is that they do not differ significantly from problems of adjustment that young people have already faced and will continue to face in both work and non-work situations. They will have already encountered similar problems of learning at school and may continue to confront similar problems of adjustment to adult behaviour in their family and leisure activities. This does not mean that the young people will not experience the adaptations or adjustments which are required as creating difficulties or problems, only that such problems will not be seen as *unusually* serious. These are the kind of everyday problems which the majority of young people face as they make the transition from school to work, but which are not seen by themselves or by those people professionally involved with them as creating special problems of adjustment to work.

Special or distinctive problems of adjustment to work occur when the adjustments required on entering work, or during the early years of the occupational career, conflict with the perspectives which are held. That is, in those situations where there is an incongruence between the young person's self-image and orientation to work on the one hand and the constraints and realities of the work situation on the other. Young people in such situations may be forced to change the ways in which they habitually think and act in relation to the world of work. It will be argued in this book that when this occurs they face a potentially traumatic situation because they may be questioning fundamental beliefs about themselves that have been built up and reinforced over a substantial number of years. This situation is epitomized by the plight of the grammar-school boy working on the production line. He will have been brought up to regard work as a central area of achievement, and to evaluate his worth in terms of success in it. Such a perspective is completely inappropriate to his position as an unskilled worker, and will create serious problems for him in that his job cannot provide him with a successful career and so he will inevitably see himself as a failure.

Most young people do not have to face traumatic situations, for in the course of their transition from school to work they enter occupations that provide support and elaboration for the self-images and orientations to work acquired during their earlier experience in the home and school. For those who do face this second type of problem of adjustment, the meaning it will have for them will differ from one group to another, in accordance with the type of self-image and orientation to work which they have developed and the situation they confront at work.

PLAN OF THE BOOK

The attempt to portray the ways in which young people see the world and their place in it is the major aim of the book because we feel that this will clarify the different problems which they experience as they make the transition from school to work. Stemming from this analysis are questions concerning both the practical provisions which are made for young people making the transition, and those concerning broader policy issues. We hope that our discussion of all these matters will be of use to both practitioners and academics.

We have distinguished three main groups which seem particularly important to an understanding of the process of transition from school to work.[3] These are each characterized by differing perspectives. The first group consists of those from 'lower' and 'middle' working-class backgrounds who enter the lower streams of the schools and enter semi-skilled and un-skilled work (see Diagram 1, p 21). These jobs provide little security and an earnings profile which quickly levels off after the early years at work and eventually declines. As they do not offer any chance of advancement or promotion we refer to them as *careerless* jobs. We consider this group in Chapter 3. The second group consists of those coming from a 'respectable working-class' background who enter the middle streams of the state school system and take up skilled manual, and lower-grade technical and clerical work. Such jobs provide more security and higher levels of salary than do careerless jobs. We refer to them as providing *short-term* careers due to the rather 'flat' career ladder of only two to four positions which they provide. We consider this group in Chapter 4. The third group is to be found among the young people coming from a 'middle-class' background who enter the higher streams of the state school system and enter similar jobs to their parents'. Such jobs are characterized by high levels of security, and salaries that increase progressively throughout most of the working life. Because of the lengthy career ladder which such jobs provide we refer to them as providing *extended* careers. We consider this group in Chapter 5. For the sake of clarity we focus upon the central groups in each of these channels, and delay consideration of those who move between these groups to the second part of the book.

In each of these three groups the meaning that the young person learns to attach to work is different. This means that the kind of situations that create problems of adjustment to work will differ from one group to another. It also means that the experience of the problems will differ significantly from one group to another. In order to clarify and demonstrate this, the first part of the book is devoted to an examination of the characteristic features of the different types of self-image and orientation to work found in these groups and the manner in which they are reinforced by the young person's experience of work. Only after this has been achieved is it possible to examine some of the problems generated by the incongruence between self-image and the 'realities' of the work situation (in Chapter 6). Finally, we examine the provisions that are made for young people in the course of their transition from school to work (Chapter 7) and the policy issues raised by our analysis (Chapter 8).

SOURCES OF INFORMATION

Before ending this introductory chapter we should say something about the nature of our sources of information. More
detailed information is provided in the Further Reading.
Chapter 2 is based on a fairly extensive body of research into
the relationships between social class, education and occupation. The evidence upon which the next four chapters are
based is drawn from interviews with young workers[4] and
published material. Due to the somewhat fragmentary nature
of the evidence, in places we have had to draw our own in-
ferences from the available material. We have drawn our
picture in fairly broad strokes in these chapters in order to
clarify the elements and processes involved, and this has inevitably meant that many of the subtle variations are glossed
over. While we are confident of the validity of our argument
there is little research bearing directly upon certain aspects of
our conceptualization. Thus, wherever we express caution in
the way in which we interpret the evidence ('the evidence
suggests', 'it seems to us') this indicates that either the status
of the evidence is unclear, or we are using theory that has not
been fully substantiated. In order to provide the reader with
some idea of the different experiences and perspectives which
we discuss in these chapters we have included specimen case
studies in an appendix. The evidence for the chapter on
agencies and policy is based on government reports, the journals of the professions involved, and discussions with people
actively involved with the problems of young people at both
national and local levels. These discussions were an important
source for our consideration of policy matters in the last chapter,
although we must stress that this chapter presents our own
views on the matter.

Notes

1   In the rest of the book we shall use the shorter term 'work' to refer to
full-time paid employment. However, we wish to make it clear that we
are fully aware that we are ignoring that sizable proportion of the
population which is in full-time unpaid work, i.e. housewives.

2   See for example M. P. Carter, *Home, School and Work*, Oxford: Pergamon Press 1962, and J. Maizels, *Adolescent Needs and the Transition from School to Work*, London: Athlone Press 1970.

3   Unfortunately we have not the space to deal with those young people who leave school at 18, nor those who are in the private sector of secondary education. We have focused on these three types because they are the most common, and are the ones which the various service agencies encounter most frequently.

4   Some of the interviews on which this book is partly based were conducted in the mid-1960s. They were part of a research project carried out in Leicester under the direction of N. Elias. The senior author (Ashton) was associated with the later phases of the project and is indebted to Professor Elias for some of his ideas. The research was carried out by Ms E. T. Kiel, Ms C. Riddell, Mr C. Tipton, Mr B. Green and Mr H. Fawcett. These data have been supplemented by work conducted by ourselves and students at the University of Leicester in recent years.

2. An Overview of Social class, Education and Occupation

In the previous chapter we briefly identified three main patterns of continuity in the experiences of young people moving into work. In this chapter we want to spell out in more detail the nature of these patterns, and to review the available information bearing on the relationships between social-class background, school and work.

SOCIAL CLASS

Diagram 1 depicts what we see to be the main ways in which family background, educational performance, and occupational choice are related at the national level. In so doing it indicates what we see as the main elements of social class. The idea of social class is central to our discussion and it is therefore important for us to explain what we mean by this term. It seems to us that social class can be broadly defined in terms of a set of relationships shared by people in similar situations. Individuals experience these relationships through their involvement in various social organizations of which the family, school and work are the most important. There are two main aspects of social class. First are those relationships which have been traditionally referred to as 'market' relationships. These 'objective' factors determine the type and level of income received and the type of work people do, and provide a set of constraints on the everyday behaviour of people. An example of this is the limitations that are imposed upon people by the nature of their qualifications and the level and regularity of the income they receive. Most people are not immediately aware of the all-pervasive influence of such factors in shaping their everyday life. The second aspect of class relationships is the

SOCIAL CLASS BACKGROUND, SCHOOL EXPERIENCE, AND 'OCCUPATIONAL CHOICE'

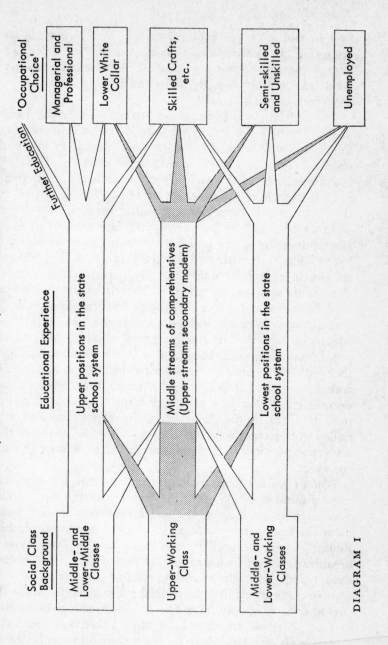

DIAGRAM I

way in which people experience their involvement in social organizations. We argue that the most important type of social organizations are work organizations, for the relationships we enter into at work directly affect the type of interactions we enter into in other areas.

The differences between these two sets of relations in their impact on the individual can be illustrated by reference to the initial choice of work. In making their 'choice' of job, young people frequently give as a reason for taking their first job features relating to the work situation, while they infrequently refer to aspects of their market situation. This is not because the latter are unimportant but rather because they are not often at the level of awareness, and are embedded in the assumptions the young people have learnt to make about the kind of person they are and the 'level' at which they will enter the labour market. For example, a young person from a middle-class family and with a grammar-school education may become a local government officer because he 'likes meeting people'. A young person from a working-class background and the lower streams of the secondary modern school who also 'likes meeting people' may choose to become a milk roundsman. Neither of them will even consider the other's choice of job as a possible way for them to 'meet people' through their work. This is because it is so 'obvious' that their respective backgrounds are pushing them in the direction of the professions and semi-skilled work respectively, that they do not think to refer to their respective positions in the labour market as reasons for choosing their jobs.

When class is conceived in this manner one can identify a core of families which carry the 'culture' of the various class groupings in our society. We will find certain families whose members from one generation to another marry people from similarly located families; who work in the same type of organizations and in the same positions within them; occupy similar positions in the education system; and live in the same type of community. It is in these families that the distinctive perspectives which we have briefly identified are transmitted and perpetuated. In addition to these families it seems that there are also families whose members over time can be seen to oscillate at the fringes of class groups. Finally, there are the genuinely mobile individuals and families who leave one class situation for another and whose children and grandchildren remain in the new class grouping or continue to be upwardly or downwardly mobile. Unfortunately sociologists have been particularly insensitive to the time dimension in the study of class.

OCCUPATIONAL STRUCTURE

The relationship between social class groupings, education and the occupational structure cannot be understood without reference to the main contours of the occupational structure. Not only does this determine the composition of these groupings, but it also determines the proportion of young people who are directed into the different types of occupation that our society has to offer.[1] Broadly speaking (all the figures that follow can only be rough approximations) the proportion of the population that is in administrative, managerial and professional careers is 17 per cent. Approximately 20 per cent are in other white-collar occupations such as clerical and junior non-manual occupations, giving a total of 37 per cent of the population (at most) in what have traditionally been referred to as middle-class occupations. Skilled craftsmen, technicians, and foremen comprise just under 30 per cent of the working population, while the semi-skilled and unskilled comprise the remaining 30 per cent. The point to be kept in mind here is that irrespective of their personal aspirations something in the region of 30 per cent of the young people in our society will enter semi-skilled and unskilled occupations in the near future, while only 17 per cent can enter managerial- and professional-type occupations.

In the following three chapters we shall explore a number of ways in which occupation affects life styles and perspectives. The most obvious factor is the nature and level of income which work provides. As Diagram 2 shows, there are dramatic differences in both the amount of income received and the income profile for each of the three groups. The careerless receive not only a significantly lower level of income but also one which declines in later life. A similar pattern occurs, but at a higher

23

level, for those in short-term careers. By contrast those in extended careers while starting at a similar level to those in short-term careers very rapidly attain significantly higher levels of income and continue to obtain further increases for most of their working life.

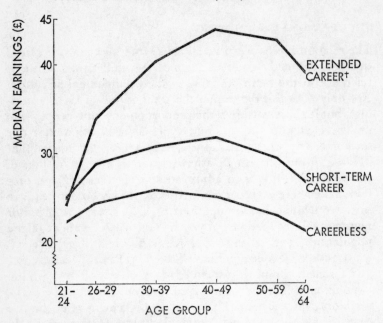

TYPICAL EARNINGS PROFILES (1970)*

*Source: Adapted from J. Westergaard and H. Resler, <u>Class in a Capitalist Society: A Study of Contemporary Britain</u> London: Heinemann 1975 p.81.

†More recent figures (the new earnings survey 1974, tables 129 & 130) indicate that the rate of income decline in extended careers is now less dramatic than indicated here.

DIAGRAM 2

If we examine the occupational distribution in a little more detail then significant differences appear in the structure of opportunities facing males as opposed to females. As the histograms show, the majority of the males in non-manual occupations are to be found in the managerial, administrative

HISTOGRAMS SHOWING THE OCCUPATIONAL DISTRIBUTION OF THE ECONOMICALLY ACTIVE POPULATION*

A: Total Active Population

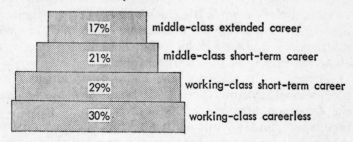

- 17% middle-class extended career
- 21% middle-class short-term career
- 29% working-class short-term career
- 30% working-class careerless

B: Male Occupations   C: Female Occupations

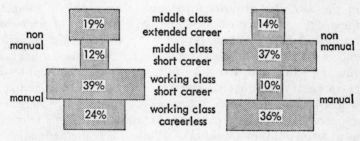

	B: Male		C: Female	
non manual	19%	middle class extended career	14%	non manual
	12%	middle class short career	37%	
manual	39%	working class short career	10%	manual
	24%	working class careerless	36%	

*Source, 1966 Sample Census

The following is a list of the socio-economic groups that comprise our categories:

Middle class extended career	1, 2, 3, 4, 5, and 13.
Middle class short career	6.
Working class short career	12, 14, 9, and 8.
Careerless	10, 11, 15, and 7.

The totals are less than 100 per cent because of the exclusion of categories 16 (armed forces) and 17 (indefinite).

DIAGRAM 3

and professional category, and within manual occupations they are mainly to be found in the skilled category. For females the opposite is the case. Within the manual occupations a majority of them are in the least skilled jobs, mainly in factory work. Within non-manual occupations the jobs open to them are confined to retail sales work and to those white collar jobs that offer few prospects for a career, such as low grade secretarial and clerical work. Teaching and nursing are the major occupations which provide an extended career to them.[2] What this means is that for females early school leaving largely precludes the chance of an extended career.

Changes in the economy have had a direct impact on the occupational structure. The most relevant of these changes to the discussion here has been the expansion of non-manual occupations, and in particular managerial, administrative, and professional occupations, together with a period of full employment since the 1950s. Associated with these changes has been a continual rise in the standard of living and associated changes in the attitudes towards work and leisure. At the moment these changes remain unexplored. Not the least of them has been that many young people have increasingly come to expect that they will obtain relatively secure employment on entering work, and that this will supply them with high levels of monetary and/or non-monetary rewards. In the 1930s school-leavers were often happy to accept *any* job, whereas it appears that from the 1960s they became increasingly selective as to *which* job they would take. While this is the national picture, it conceals important local and regional variations.

The main contrast in this respect is between on the one hand, London and the South-East, and on the other the North and North-East. The newer expanding industries tend to be located in the former region and provide the more rapidly expanding career opportunities. In the North, by contrast, are the older declining industries with fewer career opportunities, a contracting labour force, and a higher proportion of unskilled labour. The resulting differences in the demand for labour have important effects on the attitudes and aspirations of young people with regard to work. They also affect the importance of educational qualifications for entry into work. In the North and North-East where a large proportion of the jobs that are available are semi-skilled or unskilled, few young people stay on beyond the minimum school-leaving age or obtain educational qualifications. By contrast, in London and the South-East there is a greater proportion of jobs available offering careers, and more young people stay on beyond the school-leaving age and obtain the academic qualifications needed for entry into them. Paradoxically, due to the high demand for labour, young people in the South-East may find it easier than those in the North-East to enter occupations that provide a short-term career without having formal qualifications.

These differences mean that fluctuations in the level of economic activity will have different effects on young people in different parts of the country. When general economic activity declines at the national level openings for young workers will contract. In London and the South-East this may result in an increasing number of employers insisting on formal academic qualifications for entry into careers while in the North and North-East it may result in a much higher level of unemployment. In general terms it will mean that an increasing number of school-leavers will be obliged to enter occupational channels lower than those for which they were aiming. Similarly, in times of full employment and an expanding economy there may be a general upward movement as many young people who previously felt themselves destined for one specific occupational channel may find themselves with the possibility of entering a higher one.

SOCIAL CLASS, EDUCATION, AND ENTRY INTO WORK

The relationships between social class and educational opportunity and performance have been well documented in the literature.[3] It will be sufficient here to describe the main findings. Throughout the country as a whole working-class children do not perform very well in the state educational system and are excluded almost totally from the private sector. Under the old binary system, the working-class pupils were over-represented in the secondary modern schools and under-represented in the grammar schools, while children from middle-class families were over-represented in the grammar schools and under-represented in the secondary modern schools. Those working-class pupils who entered the grammar schools were not drawn evenly from the ranks of the working class but came primarily from the families of skilled manual workers, i.e. the upper stratum of the working class. While the situation varied a little from one part of the country to another, in its essentials this broad picture is fairly accurate. The introduction of comprehensive schools has done little to modify this picture, for the children from working-class families tend to predominate in the lower streams of the comprehensives while the children from middle-class families tend to predominate in the higher streams.

The relationship between the performance of young people at school and the kinds of occupation which they enter is also well documented.[4] Generally it confirms what we would expect. The children from grammar schools tend to enter middle-class or 'white collar' and professional occupations when they leave school while the children from secondary modern schools tend to enter manual occupations of one type or another.

Studies of social mobility have tended to confirm the relationships pointed to above.[5] They indicate a fairly high degree of self-recruitment within social strata. Almost all the studies indicate that the predominant direction of movement between the generations is into the same or adjacent stratum to that of the parents, and that broadly speaking about half the sons on leaving school enter the same type of work as their fathers. At first sight this may seem a surprisingly small proportion. However, it is in fact by far the largest single category of school-leavers. In the next three chapters we shall be primarily concerned with such people, while we will be concerned with some of the socially mobile school-leavers (mainly the downwardly mobile) in the following two chapters.

EDUCATION AND OCCUPATION

The relationship between the educational system and the occupational structure is in part a product of the 1944 Education Act. In recent years a number of changes in both the occupational and educational systems have occurred which require comment. As a result of the restructuring of education, from 1945 children destined for white-collar employment were separated from others and given special academic training in grammar schools. Those who failed to obtain a place in the grammar or selective schools were unlikely to obtain any certificates and were destined for manual work. Since that time there has been a number of apparently significant changes. One of these was the introduction of new forms of certification for an increasing proportion of school-leavers and the growing use by employers of these certificates in the process of selection and recruitment. During the 1950s 'Ordinary' and 'Advanced' level certificates were introduced, followed by the fairly extensive introduction of the CSE in the 1960s. The result was that it began to matter less to the employers whether or not applicants had been to a grammar school and more what 'paper qualifications' they had. Associated with this was an increasing demand by employers for some such form of qualification. The consequence of this within the secondary modern schools was the increasingly significance of the streaming and separation of those young people who were destined for some form of certification from those who were thought to be incapable of achieving this. Some measure of this tremendous increase in demand for paper qualifications is shown in Table 1. In 1971 among the older generation (i.e. over 65) 80 per cent of the males and 91 per cent of the females had no educational qualification, whereas for those between 20 and 24 years of age the proportions were 42 per cent and 51 per cent respectively.

These changes in the demand for paper qualifications and their effect on the educational system are in part a response to broader changes that have been occurring over a long period of time within the society as a whole. The increasing 'professionalization' of occupations has been a major factor contributing to the increasing emphasis on educational certification of school-leavers. Since the Second World War there has been a large increase in the number of occupations (mainly non-manual) which require some form of educational certification for entry and advancement.

29

HIGHEST QUALIFICATION LEVEL ATTAINED IN GREAT BRITAIN: SELECTED AGE GROUPS (1971)[†]

TABLE 1

Age		Males %	Females %
15-19	Higher education	0.2	0.2
	Other qualifications	45.4	41.1
	No qualifications	54.4*	58.7*
20-24	Higher education	7.5	6.7
	Other qualifications	49.8	42.9
	No qualifications	42.7	51.4
40-49	Higher education	10.7	6.7
	Other qualifications	27.2	18.9
	No qualifications	62.1	74.4
65 and over	Higher education	5.1	3.8
	Other qualifications	14.9	5.9
	No qualifications	80.0	91.3

* This table is derived from The General Household Survey Introductory Report, H.M.S.O. 1973, p. 244.

† This figure is large because it contains a substantial proportion who had not yet attempted or finished their attempt to obtain qualifications.

Three main factors may be distinguished here. First, the expansion of professions requiring a university degree or its equivalent as an entry qualification. Second, there has been a rapid growth in managerial and administrative occupations in national and local government bureaucracies and in industry which require Ordinary and Advanced General Certificates of Education as a basis for either entry and/or advancement. Finally, the Certificate of Secondary Education has become widely used as a requirement for entry into low-grade clerical and technical work. In part these factors, and especially the latter two, are linked to the increasing dominance of the economy by large organizations, and their use of 'objective' qualifications (such as educational certificates) as a means of selection and promotion. Just how far this is a product of the changing nature of the jobs or merely promotion requirements within the organization is difficult to tell at this stage.[6] In part they also relate to the attempts by a number of occupational groups to restrict entry to those who have obtained a particular level of educational certification, as part of their struggle to improve their status in society. The main result of all this has been to make educational achievement (as measured by educational certification) of central importance to the point of entry into the occupational structure.

SCHOOLS

Because of the importance which examinations have assumed they have come to play an important part in determining the internal organization of the school. Whether the system is selective or non-selective, sooner or later those young people whom the teachers see as capable of success in these examinations will be separated from those who are not deemed to be capable of such success. Sometimes this takes the form of a fairly rigid system of streaming, in others those young people who are not to be entered for external examinations are given a different, less academic and more 'interesting' curriculum. The point is that irrespective of the particular educational philosophy of the local authority or headmaster, schools have to gear themselves towards providing success in the examinations.

The status of the school as judged by employers, institutions of higher education, parents and pupils is largely based on the school's ability to produce successful candidates at examinations. This creates pressures within the school to concentrate resources on those pupils deemed likely to succeed in such examinations and in particular on the pupils being groomed for entry into higher education. In many cases the importance of the preparation of young people for examinations is all-pervasive and is seen to go well beyond the purely instrumental acquisition of qualifications, as the following comment by a headmaster illustrates:

We believe that a boy should be given the opportunity to measure his ability, his skills and his knowledge against other boys in his year and against other boys in the country. He wants to know, his parents want to know and his employers want to know where he stands in relation to his peers. . . . We as teachers want to know whether we are getting essential knowledge across to our boys. And in any case, boys love competition. Isn't all life after school competitive?

Leicester Mercury, October 17 1973

An important effect of the examination system is thus to influence materially the internal organization of the school by directing a large proportion of the school's resources towards those pupils who are being prepared for examinations. The distribution of resources is, however, not merely an internal affair. We must also consider the allocation of resources between schools. There are a number of different factors involved here, the most obvious of which is the distribution of teachers and finance between schools. Another factor, which is often over-looked, is the buildings and grounds of the school. It is well known that the older schools are located in the inner city districts which service a largely careerless population and it is these schools which have the greatest difficulty in attracting and retaining teachers. The newer grounds and better facilities are mainly found in the suburbs and in schools which cater largely for those from families in which the father has some form of career, and they are more attractive to teachers for a number of reasons. Not only are the facilities available more adequate, but these schools are likely to be larger and to offer better career prospects to teachers. In addition, the pupils at these schools are not seen as posing the problems of discipline and control which are associated with inner city schools.

The unequal distribution of teachers between schools is compounded by an unequal distribution of financial resources between them. Because of their size and facilities the newer schools tend to be more expensive to maintain and thus inevitably take a disproportionate share of the available resources. There are also inequalities stemming from the ways in which education is financed which means that in the richer areas there are more funds available for the schools. Once again the inner city schools are at a disadvantage, and on a national level so are the schools located in the North as opposed to those in the Home Counties.

A number of attempts have been made to redress these inequalities, none of which has been particularly successful. The introduction of comprehensive schools is but the latest of these, and as with the earlier introduction of secondary-modern schools, has proceeded in a slow and piecemeal manner. Initially it was thought that the replacement of the old 'élitist' system by a variety of comprehensive schools would radically alter the way in which the education system worked. The comprehensive school, it was believed, would eliminate the barriers that previously limited access to a grammar-school type of education to a small proportion of each age group, and lead to a much greater equality of opportunity by eliminating the early selection required for the binary system. This would enable those who were previously barred from an 'academic' type of education to obtain it within the comprehensive school and so to compete effectively for entry to white collar occupations. There were, of course, other advantages advocated for the comprehensive schools. (For example, the more effective use of resources that would stem from their larger size, an advantage which has materialized.) However, in our view what many expected to be their greatest advantage, the increase in the equality of opportunity through the elimination of early selection, has not materialized.[7]

Research into this area indicates that so long as the compre-

B

hensive schools maintain streaming, then their introduction brings about few changes in the aspirations of the pupils from those they would have had, had they been separated in grammar and secondary-modern schools.[8] The increasing use made by employers of national systems of educational certification imposes constraints on the comprehensive schools to separate out, in one way or another, those the teachers think are capable of obtaining such qualifications from those who are not. What this has meant in practice is that what was previously one major division within the state educational system, between those who were and those who were not destined to obtain some qualifications, has been replaced by a series of divisions *within* the comprehensive schools. Those destined for higher educational qualifications are separated from those thought capable of obtaining CSE, leaving what is now a minority destined to leave without any qualifications. The only *major* change, it seems to us, is that in the comprehensives where a less rigid system of streaming has been introduced such separation formally occurs at a later age.

The piecemeal way in which comprehensive schools have been introduced into the educational system has largely left the grammar schools and inner city schools untouched.[9] The attempt to attract (and retain) teachers to inner city schools through a manipulation of the salary structure has proved largely unsuccessful because of the difficult conditions under which such teachers work. Slum clearance has had some impact on educational inequalities but not sufficient to make a significant change in the overall pattern. Thus we suggest that despite the changes which have been made in the educational system its basic outline has remained unaltered since 1945.

PURPOSE OF THE CHAPTER

What we have been considering in this chapter are some of the 'objective' factors that are influential in shaping the ways in which people relate to each other. We make no pretence that this has been an exhaustive analysis. Our purpose has been to remind the reader that when we discuss the perspectives through which young people view their world, the factors that are in part responsible for shaping these are themselves constantly subject to change. Against this background we can now turn to examine in more detail some of the characteristic features of the educational and occupational channels that face young people and the manner in which they shape their perspectives.

Notes

1 The figures on which our discussion of the occupational structure is based are drawn from the 1966 sample census.

2 For a brief discussion of the work position of women see A. Oakley, *Housewife*, London: Allen Lane 1974, pp. 72–9. At present there is a marked absence of research into and knowledge about the perspectives and experiences of young women. This has hampered our discussion of the problems experienced by young women.

3 For a summary of the relevant literature see O. Banks, *The Sociology of Education*, London: Batsford 1976.

4 See O. Banks, op. cit., and B. Swift, 'Job Orientations and the transition from school to work: a Longitudinal Study', *British Journal of Guidance and Counselling*, Vol. 1, No. 1, January 1973.

5 See D. C. Glass (ed.), *Social Mobility in Britain*, London: Routledge and Kegan Paul 1954.

We expect that our knowledge of national mobility rates will be updated and improved when the results of the Oxford Social Mobility Research Group's survey completed in 1972 are published. In the meantime there is reason to believe that the pattern of self-recruitment found by P. M. Blau and O. D. Duncan, *The American Occupational Structure*, New York: Wiley 1967, is likely to exist in British society. For details of the pattern of self-recruitment found in the Leicester sample see D. N. Ashton, 'The Transition from School to Work: Notes on the development of different frames of reference among young male workers', *The Sociological Review*, Vol. 21, No. 1, 1973.

6 This is discussed more fully in I. Berg, *Education and Jobs*, Harmondsworth, Middx.: Penguin 1973.

7 While the 'open-ness' of the comprehensive schools has enabled some young people to obtain educational qualifications which would have been denied them under the old system this has been offset by a small loss of able pupils who are unable to cope with the open-ness of the comprehensives, and so fail to succeed in this context. See S. J. Eggleston, 'Some environmental correlates of extended secondary education in England', *Comparative Education*, Vol. 3, 1967).

8 On this point see J. Ford, *Social Class and the Comprehensive School*, London: Routledge and Kegan Paul 1969.

9 This evidence is discussed by S. J. Eggleston, 'Research and the Comprehensives', *Times Educational Supplement*, 24 January 1975, pp. 22–3.

3. The Careerless

The young people we are concerned with in this chapter are those who make the transition from the lower streams of the state schools into semi-skilled and unskilled work *without* experiencing serious problems of adjustment.[1] The majority of these young people are from families in which the parents are in careerless jobs, i.e. jobs with low levels of income which do little more than cover the basic necessities of life, and which may be subject to weekly fluctuations. Their parents will have had little formal education, and usually lack the knowledge and social skills necessary to make the most of the educational and social services formally available to them. The families are frequently of a large size and are often housed in poor and overcrowded conditions with few facilities such as books and toys for the children. This is a world in which the family frequently finds its limited resources stretched to the extreme, and the major problems are those of 'making ends meet' and of overcoming the *immediate* day-to-day problems of living. Let us now look at how these factors influence the way in which the child comes to view the world.

The most important and all-pervasive factors influencing relationships between parents and children are the market situation and work experiences of the parents, for these carry over in a variety of ways into the family situation. The most basic element of this is the nature and level of income the job provides. The weekly income derived from semi-skilled and unskilled work is of a relatively low level. It is also of a variable nature since a varying proportion of it may be based on piece-work, overtime and bonus schemes. Such incomes typically reach a peak fairly early in the work life and decline in later life. The low and variable level of income inevitably focuses attention on immediate day-to-day problems of existence and precludes long-term planning. In a very real sense these people live in a world of the 'immediate present' where their attention is confined to the recurrent problems of allocating their scarce resources. In addition to such problems, the limited financial resources severely restrict the leisure, or more accurately non-work activities, of such families. Another aspect of their market situation, which varies in significance with the state of the labour market, is the security of the jobs, for it is these jobs that are most affected in times of economic recession. This may lead to a marked reduction in their level of income, or unemployment.

Work experiences also have a significant impact on family relationships. There are two aspects of these experiences to be considered: the lack of autonomy of the workers and their subordinate position. In most semi-skilled and unskilled jobs workers have little control over how they perform their tasks, although they may be able to control, within limits, their output. The most obvious example of this lack of control is the situation of the assembly line worker. Even in those jobs where the workers can exercise a certain amount of control over how they perform their tasks (e.g. milkman, shop assistant), such control is minimal. In all semi-skilled and unskilled jobs, the workers find themselves at the bottom of the prestige and authority hierarchies. It is not simply that they have little or no voice in the decisions that are made about their work, but that they have to accept such decisions made without reference to *their knowledge* of the work situation. As we shall see, this is in marked contrast to the other types of work considered in Chapters 4 and 5.

It is often the case that both work and non-work activities, together with the relationships formed with others, are limited to those available within the relatively limited geographical area within which they reside. This often leads to the development of fairly close community bonds in such areas since non-work activities, e.g. drinking or bingo, are often shared with fellow workers who are also neighbours since most people work locally. Such communities are found primarily, but not ex-

37

clusively, in the heavily industrialized areas in the North and Midlands. Local government slum-clearance schemes may have had some impact upon this type of community. However, there is some scattered evidence to suggest that the main impact has been to separate the place of residence from the immediate work locality while not greatly undermining the relatively closed pattern of community relationships. More recent slum clearance schemes have been aimed at rebuilding in the same locality, and hence minimizing the impact of slum clearance on community bonds.

Within their families these workers appear to treat their children in similar ways to those in which they are treated at work. We suggest that this is because they have not experienced ways of exercising authority other than those where the person in authority 'lays down the law' in an attempt to control the behaviour of those under him. For example, if the father is tired the children will be told to 'shut up' without any explanation, for just as the parents are given no explanation or opportunity to answer back at work, so they expect their children to obey without question the orders given to them. In this type of family, authority is likely to be exercised not primarily by reference to general principles of behaviour, but in relation to the specific circumstances of the immediate situation. If obedience is not shown by the children then the enforcement of punishment is likely to be immediate and physical, i.e. they may be smacked or thumped if the parents can reach them. If the children can avoid punishment then the parent is likely to forget the incident. In this sense we can say that discipline in such families is arbitrary and inconsistently applied. We suggest this is an important element leading the children to relate to others not in terms of general principles of behaviour, but in terms of the constraints of the immediate situation. Whether or not they do 'shut up' is likely to depend not upon general considerations of the reasoning behind the order, but upon their perception of the chances of avoiding sanctions in the here and now. For them the rules that govern behaviour are closely tied to circumstances of the immediate situation.

The parents' experience of work is not the only factor leading to such treatment of the children. Overcrowding and family size are also important for they mean that the parents have less chance of avoiding the children when they are tired. Not only are there more children demanding attention, but there are also likely to be young children (who require a lot of attention) in the household over a long period of time. When the number of young children is compounded by the lack of rooms the problem facing the parents becomes more difficult. Even if they wished to, the parents just do not have the time to explain the whys and wherefores behind their orders. Finally, and something which is often overlooked in the literature, the problems facing the parents are further compounded by their worries about such mundane things as paying for the recurrent expenses of food, rent, utilities, and clothing for the children.

The most important effect of all this on the children is that they are brought up in a world of the 'immediate present'. What this means is that the demands of the immediate situation are so important that the children are not given the opportunity to consider the longer-term consequences of their behaviour. They have to act in a world of the here and now where actions are instantly rewarded or punished. The children thus learn to guide their behaviour with reference to such immediate considerations, and with little awareness of possible longer-term consequences.

Having considered how the children learn to act in their world, let us now look at the attitudes and expectations they develop, which are intimately connected with the 'immediate' nature of their world. They quickly learn to respond to things in terms of their 'obvious' characteristics. A good example of this is the relationship between the sexes. Boys are clearly different from girls in that they are expected to be more aggressive, noisier, and are not expected to contribute to the running of the house. Girls on the other hand are expected from an early age to help around the house and help with the younger children. They are also expected to be submissive and less enquiring. Sexual identity is also seen to be an important differentiating factor in the adult world in that here, too, males are allowed greater freedom and privileges than females, although they are expected to be the main providers for the family. Girls thus learn to see themselves primarily as prospective wives and mothers, and only secondarily as providers of income, while boys are more oriented towards the world of work and their prospective role of breadwinner.

SCHOOL EXPERIENCE

The children's experiences at school are also important in forming their attitudes and expectations. Perhaps of central importance here is that their way of looking at the world and relating to others is often at odds with that which is transmitted in the school. One of the aims of formal education, particularly at the secondary level, is to transmit an appreciation of the underlying rules and principles of knowledge as, for example, in the teaching of French, or English, or mathematics. This approach to education is inconsistent with the previous experiences and perspectives of these young people in a number of ways. First, children who have been brought up in situations where their attention is focused on the immediately apparent aspects of situations may have difficulty learning the non-apparent, underlying aspects of the discipline taught. While they may find certain aspects of their lessons interesting they may be unable to grasp the broader relevance of them. For example, they may like reading stories for English lessons, but be unable to master the exercises in English grammar or précis for which such stories form the basis. Such difficulties may result in a low level of performance as judged by the standards of the school and so lead the children to become viewed by their teachers (and other pupils) as 'thick', 'stupid', or 'lazy'. Once these definitions are established they have the effect of excluding the children from a whole range of educational possibilities: because they are 'stupid' it is assumed that they cannot be taught; because they cannot be taught there is no point in 'wasting' the school's best teachers and other scarce educational resources on them. A vicious cycle of negative definition and poor teaching is thus often established where these children are concerned. This reinforces the increasing conviction on the part of the children that their education is largely useless to them.

The kind of beliefs referred to above, and the problems arising from them, will not necessarily operate in the same way in all schools. In some schools an effort has been made to devote more of the school's resources to these children by separating them from other pupils and giving them special teachers and 'interesting' curricula. We suggest that while this strategy may mitigate some of the more negative consequences of the traditional form of streaming, it cannot entirely remove them. The very fact that they are given special teachers and non-examination-oriented curricula is sufficient to convey to them that they are not like other pupils, and that they are destined for careerless occupations. In schools where streaming is not practised, the fact that these young people are not entered for external exams will also convey their 'failure' to them.

At a general level there is disagreement between the teachers and these children and their parents as to the general value and purpose of education. As one would expect, the teachers tend to place education high on their scale of values. For them it is seen not just as a means of preparing young people for work but also, and possibly of more value, as contributing towards the general personal development of the children. These pupils in general are much more instrumental[2] in their attitude towards education and value it only in so far as it prepares and helps them get a job – which as we shall see, it achieves only in a negative sense for these young people. These differing evaluations of education reflect the more general gulf between the class perspectives of the two. From the perspective of these children and their parents, education which is aimed at 'personal development' and at preparing the child for an extended career is irrelevant. The children soon realize that such careers are not for them and come to expect (if they did not all along) that they will enter work similar to that of their parents. In this world of work they know that there is no possibility of long-term career advancement. The teachers on the other hand occupy their present position precisely because they have achieved a measure of success during a long and competitive period of training and career advancement.

Practically speaking, the tension between the children and the school is indicated to them by their allocation to the lowest streams of the school. Despite the comprehensive movement schools are still largely geared to academic success, interpreted in terms of examination performance; in this context, these children are 'failures'. While they do not necessarily see themselves as failures they do come to see themselves as 'not good at school' and 'not brainy', and begin to accept the image of limited ability which is transmitted to them by the attitudes of their teachers and by the 'successful' pupils. In the majority of schools where streaming, or a modified form of streaming operates, the children in the lower streams do tend to develop negative attitudes towards school or at best a noncommittal attitude. Studies in different parts of the country have noted that these children tend to see their teachers as 'not interested in us' and 'only interested in the brainy ones'. This negative attitude is not just confined to the teachers but is also generalized to the subjects taught. The growing awareness on the part of these children of their 'failure' within the school, and the associated realization of the irrelevance of much of what they do at school for the kind of work for which they are destined, is, one suspects, a gradual process.

From the parents' point of view the placing of their children in the lowest streams may merely confirm what they always expected. After all, they were no good at school, why should their children be different? Further, as they expect their children to enter jobs similar to their own, they are likely to see their education as of minor importance. There is thus little incentive for them to take an interest in their children's education or to visit the school and consult teachers – which confirms the teachers' view of the parents as failing to provide support or interest in the children. Even where the parents are interested in helping the child it is likely that their educational background will prevent them from being able to do so. There are other disincentives for these children besides the lack of parental support. In particular, overcrowding and large family size make it difficult for most of these children to concentrate on their homework in the way necessary for success at school.

As these children progress through the secondary schools they become increasingly disillusioned with their teachers and bored with their lessons. This poses problems both for them and for their teachers. The children are faced with the problem of coping with lessons which are seen as boring and useless, and often resort to 'messing around' or truancy as solutions. They are thus likely to come into conflict with their teachers. The teachers are faced with the problems of control, which frequently lead them to use physical punishment and detentions as the only sanctions the children will understand. While these may provide an effective means of maintaining quiet and order, they are experienced by the children as an example of the arbitrary way in which teachers act towards them. The school may thus become little more than a custodial institution for these children as far as both they and their teachers are concerned, and their behaviour becomes determined by the necessity to avoid punishment and to 'get by' with as few 'aggravations' as possible. In this latter respect their experience at school is similar in many ways to that at home, for once again their behaviour is guided by the demands of the immediate situation and not by general rules which apply across a range of situations. They are concerned with how particular teachers react towards them and how much they can 'get away with' rather than with learning about the subjects which are being taught. With the raising of the school-leaving age to 16 the frustrations which these young people experience at school are likely to become intensified.

It is well documented that by the end of their school life these children have come to see formal education as irrelevant to them. In some cases the noncommittal and negative attitudes towards school lead to outright rejection of school and all it stands for. Thus while for most the messing around and persistent rule-breaking at school represent no more than ways of relieving monotony, for others they represent a complete rejection of school and its values. This latter group are likely to be those whom 'failure' at school threatens most. Receiving only negative support at school they turn to their friends for support in their counter-rejection of the school. For them the deliberate flouting of school rules, receiving punishment at school, dressing in a manner known to cause offence to teachers, and participation in 'delinquent' activities outside school, are a source of pride and achievement in the eyes of themselves and their friends. Moreover, given their relationship with teachers

43

and other pupils, these activities may be the only source of achievement and pride that is open to them.

It must be stressed that not all the young people who develop the perspective that we are concerned with in this chapter are members of this 'delinquent sub-culture', for many exhibit no more than a mild indifference to school and are supported in this by their peer group. The activities of this latter type of group are more confined to hanging around coffee bars and street corners, and listening to music. We are not yet clear as to what it is that makes some of the young people opt for the 'delinquent solution' and not others; what is fairly obvious, however, is that the peer group which stresses anti-academic values does offer one solution to the problems that face young people moving through these positions within British society.

At this point it is appropriate to comment briefly on the problems facing the children of immigrants. Most of these children are to be found in the group we are discussing here, and in the 'problem group' discussed in Chapter 6. They experience the same types of problems we have been discussing so far, but additionally their situation is made worse by three other factors. The first, and most obvious, is that they often have difficulty at school because of their poor command of the English language. Second, there is often an even greater discrepancy between their beliefs and values and those held by their teachers and the other children at school. This is particularly the case for many Asian immigrants, and especially for Asian girls. Finally, these children often suffer from discrimination at both the personal and institutional levels. At school they are often discriminated against by both other pupils (including other immigrant groups) and teachers. Moreover, as schools with a large proportion of immigrant pupils are located predominantly in inner city areas, they are less likely than other schools to be allocated scarce educational resources and are less likely to be able to attract good teachers.

Their experiences at school have important consequences for the ways in which all these children view the world and themselves. In many ways they reinforce the perspectives initially developed in the family. In particular they reinforce their concern with and focus on the 'immediate present' as the main source of gratification and frustration. In contrast to other pupils in the school, for these children there are no future rewards arising from their school work. There is no promise or even hope of their acquiring educational certificates, and because they are in the lowest streams little chance of a 'good' school-leaving report. The only rewards and satisfactions that they can hope to obtain from their school life are those that can be obtained from the here and now. Yet even here the satisfactions are few, for the academic subjects are of little interest to them, and their teachers frequently regard them as incapable of further development. School life, particularly in the later years, thus becomes a question of filling in time.

Other aspects of the perspectives acquired within the home are also reinforced by experiences at school. As was the case within the family, so too at school, the relationships they enter into give them little scope or discretion, for here too they are in an inferior status position. The definition of them as academically inferior means that they are provided with little chance to develop their academic skills beyond a minimal level. Their common failure in the majority of school subjects and the limited chances they have to develop interests and competence in other practical and sporting activities provide them with few opportunities to develop feelings of confidence and pride in themselves. The main exception to this is that girls are frequently encouraged to develop their skills in cookery and mothercraft, which further reinforces their notion of themselves as destined primarily for housework.

ENTRY INTO WORK

The 'objective' and 'subjective' consequences of the children's (especially boys') 'failure' at school interact when it comes to their choice of work. Allocation to the lowest streams not only has the 'subjective' consequences discussed above, but also has 'objective' results. As a result of their allocation to the lowest streams they are no longer expected to perform well in academic subjects nor to develop more than very minimal skills. Thus, they are not given the chance to develop the kind of skills that are often seen as necessary for entry into anything other than semi-skilled and unskilled work. In this sense allocation to the lowest streams acts as a barrier against entering apprenticeships or other types of highly skilled work.[3] It should be noted that these young people are committed to a future in careerless occupations not as a result of their own conscious decisions or those of others, but rather as a result of the unintended consequences of the organization of the school.

Irrespective of the pleasure or hostility with which the last few years of school are experienced, these young people learn to see themselves as only fit for semi-skilled and unskilled occupations. By the end of their school career they predictably make choices within this group of occupations. Moreover, while these are the jobs that others regard as 'dead end' and do their utmost to avoid, these young people are often positively looking forward to entering them, for their school experiences provide a background against which work of a routine and fragmentary kind can be regarded as providing freedom and independence.

The way in which these young people obtain information about the jobs they consider entering has often been seen as haphazard. We suggest that this is not the case, and that this view results from a failure to recognize the network of 'informal' (i.e. 'non-professional') sources of information available to these young people. The information that these young people acquire about the local labour market is obtained primarily by word of mouth from family, friends, and relatives, for these people are actively involved in the local labour market and are likely to know, either directly or through their friends, what jobs are available. Failing this, they can always follow the time-honoured practice of going round from firm to firm in the locality and asking about possible vacancies. The main reason for relying on such informal networks is that the information derived from friends and neighbours is often seen as more reliable and useful than that which they can obtain from 'official sources' such as careers officers who have no direct experience of the semi-skilled and unskilled labour market and who are dependent on employers for their knowledge of it. Indeed, because of their lack of direct experience these agents may be unable to appreciate the subtle differences between such jobs. By the time they leave school most of these young people have developed an appreciation of a number of meaningful differences between the jobs available to them. Not only are there monetary differences, but such factors as working inside or outside, the degree of independence the job allows, and the distance from home are also seen as important. Factors such as these become the principal means by which young people distinguish between jobs.

The point to be noticed about these factors is that they are not such as to commit the young person to any one specific job. From their point of view, the young people have learnt not to expect a great deal from work activities apart from satisfactions that can be derived from the here and now. If what is wanted is an outside job, then there are several which are suitable, e.g. van boy, delivery boy, builder's labourer, and it may not matter which of these jobs they enter. In some cases there will be no positive job requirements, only negative ones, e.g. an aversion to factory work or getting up 'at the crack of dawn'. Thus what may appear to some as a casual and haphazard way of choosing a job is in fact perfectly understandable given the previous experiences and the future expectations of these young people. So long as the labour market is favourable, then if they do not like the job they first enter, they can always move on, for theirs is not a lifetime commitment to a 'career'.

WORK EXPERIENCE

On their entry into work many of these young workers are somewhat apprehensive, and sometimes the behaviour of older workers may cause initial disquiet. This initial apprehension is only to be expected as it is a normal characteristic of entry into any new situation. Most of these young people, however, settle down to the routine of work with relative ease although the boredom, lack of autonomy and authority, and the careerless character of these jobs almost inevitably take their toll. As they become more acutely aware of these limitations of their jobs, the boys especially increasingly adopt a more critical attitude towards them. For the girls this disillusionment may not be felt so acutely as they have marriage and a family to look forward to in the near future. The longer these young people stay in their careerless occupations, the more difficult it is for them to leave them and enter a different occupational channel. The age limitations for apprenticeships and the reluctance of employers to take on older workers for training make it increasingly difficult for the young workers who have spent three to four years in semi-skilled work to leave it. The result is that the young workers are further 'locked' into a future in careerless occupations. From their point of view, it means that no matter how hard they work or how conscientious they are they have little or no chance of 'getting on in life', or of 'improving themselves' in the way in which other young workers can. Although they are prevented from making a career, the careerless nature of their work allows a number of job changes to be easily made within the semi-skilled and unskilled channel. Many observers have viewed such frequent job changing as a sign of immaturity or a failure to adjust, whereas, on the contrary, for these young people it may be a perfectly realistic response to their situation. Because they have made few commitments to their job there is little to hold them to it should they become dissatisfied, for there are numerous other jobs that potentially offer the same or better rewards. For them job changing provides a means of escape from problems such as low pay, undesirable work or workmates, or problems with supervisors which may otherwise confront them for the foreseeable future.

There are, of course, many different types of careerless occupations. We have already mentioned several such as the van boy, the factory operative, the labourer, and the warehouse boy. However, a more fundamental distinction is emerging between those careerless occupations in the small firms and the service industries (where in fact most of the young workers first gain their work experience) and the careerless occupations in the larger firms. Unlike the smaller firms where little or no training is given and the young person may have to leave when his labour is no longer cheap, the larger firms tend to be more selective in their recruitment policy and are more likely to invest in some training for the new entrants, even if it is only of a rudimentary kind. The young worker entering the larger firm is thus given not only greater security but also the chance to invest time and energy in developing some of his interests. However, in both cases the young worker has little or no chance of occupational advancement, despite the greater opportunities available in the larger firms with more 'advanced' policies.

What this means for these young people is that their world of work is not one in which they can 'make something of themselves' in the sense in which the young apprentice or the young person starting as a trainee in a bank can. Work is not an area in which they can achieve membership of prestigious occupational groups; nor does it enable them progressively to improve their economic and social position as a result of their individual effort. If they do not have career expectations, we must realize that in their positions such expectations would be at best irrelevant and at worst the cause of numerous problems. They may appreciate that young workers in other occupational channels are in better jobs, but realize that these are beyond their reach. The stress that is placed on making a career by the media, as well as by teachers and careers officers, is irrelevant to these young people. This is not to argue that these young people would not hold such a belief about the value of getting on in work if their situation was changed and they were offered the chance to 'get on', but so long as they are denied that chance it is potentially disturbing for them to hold such beliefs.

The fact that work does not, in itself, hold the same value for these young people as it does for others must not be interpreted to mean that it is unimportant to them. The main importance of work is that it provides the material basis for leisure activities through their wages, and sometimes through the provision of leisure facilities such as Works sports and social clubs. Further, many friendships originate from the work relationship and carry over into shared non-work activities. In addition to these aspects of their work, young people may derive satisfaction from other aspects of their work activities such as a relative freedom from supervision, good workmates,[4] or working outside. We should emphasize that such satisfactions are primarily unconnected to the tasks they perform at work and so do not bring about much involvement in their work. (This is in marked contrast to the experience of the young workers we consider in the next two chapters, whose work does provide a basis for such involvement.) While the various factors referred to above provide a certain degree of satisfaction with their present jobs in relation to other careerless jobs, work as an area of activity in itself is not as a whole highly valued.

Work affects the perspectives of these young workers, mainly by reinforcing the experiences at home and at school. Their orientation to the here and now is reinforced in their jobs as they are once again in a situation in which they are working only for immediate rewards, for there is very little chance of promotion, no matter how hard they work. The tasks that they are engaged upon tend to be simple and repetitive, and are not tasks in which they can develop much interest. Neither are they tasks that provide scope for initiative, for they are closely circumscribed by the employers with regard to the execution of the tasks and/or the manner in which they are organized. These young people are thus once again in positions where they have to do what others say without being able to question or change matters significantly. The behaviour of these young workers is regulated in ways similar to those used in their home and the school. There are few positive incentives to comply with the rules that govern work behaviour, and the emphasis is once again on the use of negative sanctions, this time in the form of the sack or reduced earnings. As the firm cannot hold out the promise of promotion as an incentive to comply with the rules it can only punish what is regarded as non-compliance, although once again the sanctions are not imposed systematically. Finally, the ideas of themselves developed in the family and at school are also likely to be reinforced by their work experiences. Once again they are in positions in which the tasks they have to perform make minimum demands on their abilities, and they are given little or no opportunity to establish pride in their work. In this way the self-image of limited ability transmitted at school is confirmed by the failure of the jobs to provide the opportunity for the development of their abilities, and by the frequently held ideas that those who enter such 'dead end' jobs do so because they are not fit or capable of doing anything else. They thus turn to non-work activities to provide the main source of satisfaction and 'meaning' in their lives. This seems to be especially true of the young women who are likely to view their work almost entirely in an instrumental way, and are much more concerned with their eventual marriage and family.

NON-WORK ACTIVITIES

Even in their out of work activities these young people tend to be starved of facilities, especially when we compare them with those that are provided for the young people in other occupational channels. When they have sufficient money their activities are centred around the dance halls, coffee bars, and for some the youth clubs. For the older ones the pubs and working-men's clubs, cars and motor-bikes become the focus of their activities. When the money runs out in the course of the week, as it frequently does, then they are left to find their entertainment in the streets. In many ways their expenditure patterns reflect their priorities, and they tend to spend all their money on such immediate pleasures as records, cars, going out with the opposite sex, clothes, football matches, pictures, dancing and drinking.[5] These represent their major interests in life and provide the main sources for meaningful relationships with others. The pursuit of such pleasures takes place largely with people of the same background. Hardly any of them attend night classes, having had sufficient taste of 'education' at school, and many find youth clubs of little use.

It is of no surprise to find that it is from among these young people that recruits for 'skin heads', 'Hell's Angels' and other gangs are predominantly drawn. In this respect, this aspect of the so-called youth culture plays an important part in providing a focus and a meaning for the activities of the young workers that cannot be found in their school or work activities, by providing them with important sources of self-esteem through their distinctive dress and group behaviour. The final point to be made about the leisure activities of these young people is that they are again, as one would predict, focused on providing excitement and rewards in the here and now. For many of them they provide the one area in which value is attached to the opinions which others have of their worth as persons.

SUMMARY

The young people we have described are those from families in the lower and middle working class. At home they are used to living in a world of the 'immediate present' in which little thought or concern is or can be given to the future, and in which little value is placed on formal education. These are the young people who find the greatest gap between the values and standards that govern their experience in the family and those they are exposed to at school. Hence they experience a considerable clash between the culture of the home and that of the school. They are allocated to the lowest streams in the school, and are neither expected, nor provided with the opportunity, to develop their cognitive and manipulative skills. Within the school they are regarded as failures, as of very limited ability and as incapable of making anything of themselves. Many of these children respond to this situation by rejecting the dominant values within the school, while nevertheless accepting the image of themselves as having very limited ability. They may not necessarily see themselves as failures, since from their point of view they have never had the chance to succeed, but they do see themselves as bad at school subjects. In terms of their orientation to the world, their experience of school merely reinforces the attitudes transmitted within the family, for these young people (unlike others) are not offered any future rewards for successful performance; there are no educational certificates for them. The only rewards they can seek are those that can be obtained in the here and now, i.e. either from some intrinsic interest in the subject matter or, more likely, from just 'messing about'. Because they learn to see themselves as having limited ability they do not always consider themselves suitable for jobs that require considerable training, while their orientation to the here and now means that they are concerned with the immediate rewards that can be obtained from work rather than those that can be obtained in the future. This concern, together with their desire to leave behind what for many was an unpleasant school experience, usually results in these young people choosing to enter semi-skilled and unskilled work.

For these young people their entry into work and their early experience of it reinforce the self-image and orientation to work acquired at home and school. The only rewards their work activities can provide them with are those that can be obtained in the here and now, so that factors such as the kind of activities involved in the job, whether it is inside or outside work, and the amount of income it provides become all important. Their work provides them with little or no chance of promotion or advancement and consequently little or no chance of obtaining a substantially higher level of income in the future. The lack of scope provided by work and the often fragmented and routine nature of the work activities reinforce the image the young people have of themselves as having limited abilities. Because they have few opportunities to develop skills in which they can take some pride, they have little chance to think of themselves as capable of performing the more complex activities associated with other types of occupation. For them, work is something that has to be done in order to acquire the resources necessary to enjoy non-work activities. There are, of course, certain sources of satisfaction that can be found in semi-skilled and unskilled work, but work is not an area which provides many achievements, and their major interests and their more meaningful activities are to be found outside work.

Given the nature of the work they are doing and their earlier experiences in the home and school, it is not at all surprising that these young people do not accept the dominant beliefs that it is important to have a career, or that work should be an area in which you 'make something of yourself'. Some of these young workers reject these and similar beliefs as irrelevant to them, while others, as they had done at school, invert the dominant beliefs and maintain that occupations that provide careers are to be avoided, and place a higher value on semi-skilled and unskilled jobs because they do not tie them down and restrict their freedom of movement.

When these young people come to establishing their own families the processes which we have discussed in this chapter are likely to be perpetuated.

Notes

1 As we shall see (in Chapter 6) not all young people entering such occupations find the transition from school to work unproblematic. It is difficult to be precise but it seems that just under one-half of the males and a small minority of females entering what we have termed careerless occupations experience serious problems. Given the apparent 'objective undesirability' of these jobs it is perhaps surprising that such a *small* proportion of them experience difficulties.

2 By instrumental we mean an attitude whereby the activity in question is not valued for its own intrinsic worth or satisfaction but as a means to an end or ends external to that activity.

3 As long as the secondary-modern school did not push its more able pupils into external examinations it was difficult for employers to discriminate between pupils, and there is some evidence to suggest that allocation to the lower streams was not as powerful a determinant of subsequent occupational careers as it is now. As educational certificates become increasingly important for access to jobs offering short-term careers, so the system of streaming becomes more important in determining the chance the pupil has for acquiring these certificates and consequently for entering this type of employment. However, regional variations in occupational opportunities will have some effect on this, as we have pointed out in Chapter 2.

4 For women the evidence shows that good workmates clearly provide the main source of job satisfaction, whereas for men this is but one among a number of factors.

5 We are not claiming that other types of young people have radically different patterns of interest and expenditure. However, they play a different part in their lives and do not seem to consume all their non-work time and expenditure. For example, they are more likely to save money than these young people. Other differences will be indicated in the following chapters.

4. Short-term Careers

In this chapter we are concerned with those young workers who enter occupations which offer short-term career prospects. The occupations we have in mind are skilled manual trades, technical occupations (e.g. Post Office engineers), and certain types of clerical and secretarial work.[1] The majority of these young people come from families whose parents are in such jobs, and move through the middle levels of the state school system (i.e. the upper streams of secondary-modern schools and the middle streams or 'sets' of the comprehensive schools). In contrast to the young people discussed in the previous chapter there are a number of important differences in their pre-work experiences, the effect of which is to free them from an overwhelming concern with the 'immediate present' and to direct their attention to the short-run future consequences of actions.

As with the careerless group, the market situation and work experiences of the parents influence family life in a number of important ways. Once again the income received from work is important. Although the resources of these families are frequently stretched, their income is regular, dependable, and sufficient to meet day-to-day recurrent expenses. In addition, the level of income has some possibility of a real increase. This serves to free the family from the chronic anxiety associated with 'making ends meet' found in lower income families, and allows a degree of short-term planning.

The pattern of work relationships is also important. Unlike the semi-skilled and unskilled workers, these workers have a limited but significant degree of control over the way they perform their work. This stems partly from the nature of the work tasks, the execution of which demands skill and expertise, and

55

often a lengthy period of training. A second source of such control by the workers over their work is the way in which they are viewed by those in authority; namely as 'fairly well educated', intelligent people who are capable of getting on with their work without close supervision. Although the degree of autonomy will vary from job to job, one consequence of this expertise is that those in authority cannot dictate the way in which jobs are to be performed, nor how long they should take, in nearly as precise a way as they can for unskilled work. All this is not to say that the employees have complete freedom at work, for the area over which they can exercise control is clearly limited by rules laid down by the employing organizations. This limited freedom at work is, however, frequently a source of satisfaction for these workers, and often leads to a sense of achievement and self-esteem which is largely lacking for those in semi-skilled and unskilled work. Further, their mastery of the skills required for the execution of often complex tasks provides another possible source of pride and achievement.

It is difficult to be precise about the exact way in which these work experiences carry over and influence parent-child relationships due to the variety of experience at work in such occupations. Similarly, the types of community relationships are also variable. In some cases they are very similar to those described in the previous chapter; i.e. where work and non-work activities are shared, as is the case with the shipbuilding trades. In other cases there are no such close community bonds, and work and non-work relationships tend to be more clearly separated. In such cases, while work may provide one course of friendships these tend to be specific to only a few people and are not shared by the work group as a whole. We stress, then, that there is more variability in parent-child relationships than may appear to be the case from the following account.

The most significant difference from the pattern of parent-child relationships described in the previous chapter is that the children, and especially the boys, are allowed a certain amount of freedom within clearly defined limits set down by their parents. That is, they are treated in a way similar to that in which their parents are treated at work. There tend to be clear and fundamental rules which govern the children's behaviour, and which are explained to the children and enforced in a firm and consistent manner. Discipline in areas which are not covered by such rules is, however, likely to be more arbitrary and inconsistent. A second important difference is that the children are more frequently treated as responsible individuals (rather than simply as children) than is the case in the career-less families, although here, too, this is more frequent for boys than for girls.

The children's experiences in these families leads them to develop certain ways of looking at the world and their place in it, and although there are clear similarities between their perspectives and those described for the careerless there are important differences. Like the children from the lower income families they are brought up in a world where age and sex are important determinants for distinguishing between people. Like them they learn that boys are aggressive and girls are passive, and that men are 'breadwinners' while women are primarily 'home-makers'. The main differences result from the fairly consistent application of clear rules governing their behaviour in the family, which gives a greater degree of predictability to their world than is found in the lower income families. It means that the children can take account of these constraints and so plan their behaviour around them; thus they are not so dominated by the demands of the present because they can, to a certain extent, predict the demands ahead of time and adjust their behaviour accordingly.[2] This planning ahead is allowed not only by the clarity of the rules governing such behaviour, but also by the greater material resources available to those families, and the greater freedom children are given by their parents. All this has important consequences for the way in which the children view themselves, and is likely to lead them to develop a sense of self-determination and an awareness of the consequences of their actions for others. They are also likely to develop their own particular interests across a much greater range than the children in lower income families; this again being facilitated by the families' greater material resources.

This type of parent-child relationship is made possible by a number of the features mentioned above. The secure and consistent source of income sufficient to meet the cost of basic necessities relieves the parents of many of the anxieties which beset the lower income families, and so allows them more 'emotional energy' for their children. Further, there are likely to be fewer children demanding attention, which means that there is potentially more time to spend on each child. The important result of these two factors is that the parents are more able to get to know the individual quirks of their children, and to take an interest in and allow for them in planning family activities. Just as the nature of the income allows short-term planning of the budget, it also allows the planning of family leisure activities. This becomes another source of control over the children because their behaviour can be rewarded or punished in terms of activities such as outings which occur in the foreseeable future. The children are thus encouraged to look beyond the immediate consequences of their actions and consider longer-term consequences.

SCHOOL EXPERIENCE

A substantial proportion of children from this type of background are placed in the middle levels of the state school system where the resources of the schools are devoted to the development of their potential. As a result of their upbringing these children face fewer problems at school than those we discussed in the last chapter. While they may not be fond of the content of their lessons they are used to looking beyond the immediate context for underlying principles and hence experience less difficulty with lessons. In so far as the school lays down clear guidelines for their behaviour the children are able to work within them, since this is similar to the way in which their behaviour is guided in the home. The main area where the children are likely to experience some degree of conflict with the teachers is over the value of education. The children and their parents are likely to evaluate the subjects taught in instrumental terms and to distinguish between such subjects as mathematics and metalwork which are interesting and useful for the children's future life and those such as music and history which are seen as irrelevant and possibly resented as an attempt to impose 'culture' upon them. Similarly, the teachers' view of education as developing the 'fully rounded personality' is seen as irrelevant. However, in spite of these conflicts there is a considerable overlap between the way in which they learn to relate to others at home and at school. These young people can operate within the school context with some success and are viewed favourably by their teachers.

There are a number of consequences resulting from the allocation of these children to the middle streams of the state school system. While it is a clear indication to them of their 'superiority' over those in the lower streams whom they may come to view as 'thick' and 'stupid', at the same time it is also an indication that they are not as bright or successful as those in the higher streams. Another consequence of their position within the school is that they are viewed by their teachers in a different way to those in the lower streams. While they are not regarded as brilliant they are nevertheless seen as reasonably intelligent and capable of making some use of their education. Also, as they are more likely to accept the teachers' authority, they present few problems of control for the teachers and are seen as easier to teach. They are more likely to be allocated the 'better' teachers and other resources of the schools than those in the lower streams. The net result is that while these children come to see themselves as of only 'average' ability they also see themselves as reasonably intelligent and capable of developing their special interests and skills at school.

We do not intend to suggest that these young people un-critically accept the teachers' definitions of them. Indeed many of them will consider the 'culture' of the school irrelevant and believe that their teachers have little idea of the 'real' world which exists outside the confines of the school. However, their position in the school provides support for the belief that they have the sort of qualities which prospective employers are looking for, and that they can obtain the necessary qualifications for entry into 'good' jobs. Thus while they may reject certain aspects of school life, they nevertheless are likely to agree with their teachers about the importance of doing well at school, although for more pragmatic reasons.

The effects of their allocation to the middle levels of the state educational system were much clearer under the old selective system where failure in the 11-plus was a clear indication of their lack of success relative to those entering grammar schools, while their allocation to the highest streams of the secondary-modern school was an equally clear indication of their superior status as compared to those in the lower streams. Under the comprehensive system, and with the increasing use by the larger employers of educational certificates as a necessary qualification for entry into apprenticeships, etc., the process by which the young people become aware of the ceiling to their 'career ambitions' may be much more gradual. It may only be after their allocation to a particular band or group in preparation for their school-leaving certificate that they are confronted with the fact that they are being denied access to a number of jobs which they may at an earlier stage have considered desirable, a situation which occurs without their making a conscious decision about their choice of occupational channel. But for the majority, coming from the families of manual workers, this may not be unexpected since they may never have considered entry to managerial or professional work as anything other than fantasies.

An important consequence of their position at school is that it reinforces their tendency to subordinate the consideration of immediate rewards for more general short-term rewards. Unlike the careerless, these children have a number of incentives which encourage them to do this. For them school has something more to offer than just elementary skills in reading and writing. As we have suggested, it offers a series of academic and practical skills that will provide access to and training for some of the 'better' (more highly skilled and paid) occupations. In providing these opportunities it allows them to develop their interests and more practical abilities, which in turn provide them with a source of pride and achievement. Also, because they can understand the general principles which are being transmitted, they are able to do better in their subjects and so are more likely to receive praise from their teachers for their work. In the later years of school the short-term rewards associated with successful performance in their final examinations, namely the near certainty of entry into those jobs that provide a short-term career, become important.

As at home these rewards associated with school work act as an incentive for the children to comply with the basic rules of conduct of the school. In school, there are a number of clear and unambiguous rules that are used to establish and define good behaviour, and within which the young persons have a certain degree of autonomy or control over their own behaviour. As at home there are certain sanctions (that are not available to the teachers of the careerless) that are fairly consistently used to punish transgression of the basic rules. Perhaps the most important of these is the threat of demotion to a lower stream with all that this implies in terms of the reduction of the child's status and, especially later, its chances in the labour market. In this context it is worth noting that the main problem these children will experience at school is not boredom with their lessons (as is the case with the careerless) but that of mastering the academic and practical skills necessary for academic success and the rewards that this will bring. Their parents are likely to play an important role here by encouraging the children to work at their school subjects because they can see the significance of success at school for their children's chances of obtaining a 'good job'. We suggest that one of the consequences of the 'openness' of some comprehensives is to reduce the impact of the signals from the school about pupils' abilities, and thereby to increase the importance of parental attitudes.

As they move towards the end of their school days these young people do not experience the outright rejection of the school that is characteristic of many of the young people in the lower channel. For the majority of them, the last year at school tends to be a fairly pleasant experience. As in many cases they tend to stay beyond the minimum leaving age, and as the last year is often seen as the culmination of their earlier efforts, the raising of the school-leaving age has not presented them with many problems. Although their experience of school may be satisfactory they look forward to leaving, for, in accordance with their instrumental evaluation of education, they realize that school has little more to offer them that is relevant to their future employment. Hence work, with the independence and freedom it promises and the income they know it will provide, becomes more attractive. Many appreciate the value of staying on at school for those aiming at entry into extended careers, but see themselves as having reached their limit. This is as true for those who identify closely with the school, hold positions of responsibility within it (e.g. prefect) and are involved in many extracurricular activities as it is for those who are indifferent or hostile to school.

ENTRY INTO WORK

When deciding about work their 'objective' educational situation interacts with the ideas they have formed of themselves to steer these young people towards a certain range of jobs. Their self-image is such that they refuse to consider unskilled and semi-skilled work since such jobs as factory operative, shop assistant or labourer are all considered as 'dead end jobs' and only fit for those who can do no better. What they are concerned with when seeking a job is to find one that enables them to 'make something of themselves' and to 'get somewhere in life'. In order to obtain these objectives they are prepared, as their earlier experiences have taught them, to forgo the higher wages that could be obtained immediately in semi-skilled work and to accept lower wages during their period of training. While they are also sensitive to other 'immediate' rewards of work when seeking a job, such rewards are not given the main priority in choosing between jobs, and what is given most significance is whether the job provides prospect for the future. The evaluation of such prospects is usually based on whether the job offers security of employment and the chance to acquire some sort of skill which will provide relatively high income and status in the near future. Their educational qualifications, however, are such as to prevent them from entering professional and managerial careers which meet these requirements, even if these were ever considered.[3] For the boys, entry to apprenticeship is the traditional way of meeting such requirements, although there are a range of other jobs which also provide such short-term career prospect

For girls only hairdressing is formally structured in terms of apprenticeship and their other alternatives are mainly restricted to State Enrolled nursing and to office work such as telephony and secretarial work, which provide transferable skills.

The importance of educational certification for entry into occupations which provide short-term careers varies for two main reasons. Firstly, there are differing entrance requirements to such jobs. For example, entry into technician apprenticeships is usually impossible without CSE or GCE 'O' level educational certification, whereas the entry requirements for craft apprenticeships are usually not as stringent. Second, as we have pointed out, the extent to which formal entrance requirements are adhered to may vary greatly with the state of the economy and from one region to another.

The way in which these young workers set about finding their first job differs in important ways from the methods employed by those entering careerless jobs. These young people, because they have an investment in their education, frequently wish to make the best of it and so seek information on the kind of jobs that are available in their locality more systematically than the careerless. If they fail to find the kind of job they seek they are reluctant to accept a careerless job, for this would mean that not only would they have 'wasted' their education but also that they may encounter considerable problems in adjusting to work. Given the kind of market for which they are aiming, and the importance they attach to securing a skill, these young people tend to use the more formal agencies such as their careers teachers, the youth employment service, and the local press more frequently than the other young workers entering careerless jobs. These formal agencies are more likely to know about the openings available in the larger firms because these have formal systems of recruitment and selection whereas the smaller firms with only a few openings are less likely to have formal systems of recruitment. However, this general picture tends to conceal important variations. One source of variability will be the extent of the knowledge which careers officers have obtained about the local market. Further, some of these young people obtain their jobs through the informal sources of parents, friends and neighbours. This situation, however, is likely to be far more prevalent among those who fail to obtain any educational qualifications and hence are excluded from entry to the larger firms. For them the only way in which they can hope to obtain an apprenticeship or its equivalent is through contacts which their friends, relatives and parents may have with others in the local labour market.

While in their 'choice' of job the consideration of short-term future rewards takes precedence over the immediate rewards of work, it does not enable these young people to discriminate between the various jobs that are available. The specific job they try to enter is frequently chosen with reference to immediate satisfactions that can be derived from the day-to-day activities involved in the work, in much the same way as those entering careerless jobs discriminate between the various jobs that are available to them. For some their preference for outside work leads them to choose within the building trades; for others an interest developed at school or at home in woodwork may lead them to be carpenters or joiners; while for others it is their interest in electricity that leads them to become apprentice electricians. In many cases, however, the initial choices do not materialize and so they then tend to seek work in related trades. What is significant in this context is that the immediate satisfactions sought for do not lead them to consider entering semi-skilled jobs which would meet these requirements. For example, a young person who wished to work with machines may become a fitter or toolmaker, but it is very unlikely that he would consider a job as a capstan lathe operator. If, as is occasionally the case, there are no openings in jobs that are directly linked to their immediate interests, then they would rather abandon the attempt to derive that kind of satisfaction and seek a trade in a different field altogether. The immediate satisfactions, if it comes to a choice, are invariably subordinated to short-term future requirements.

WORK EXPERIENCE

There are a number of important characteristics of this type of work. The first of these is the nature of the income. We have already discussed the significance of the provision of a regular and dependable income for the older workers with reference to the family. In the initial stages, however, the comparatively low level of income may pose problems for some young workers by restricting their leisure activities.

A more relevant characteristic for these young people is the lengthy period of training. This means that their entry into work does not mark the end of their educational career, for not only do many of them continue in part-time further education, either sponsored by their firms or of their own accord, but the early years at work are themselves regarded as a training period. One possible consequence of this continuation of education is that it may make the transition from school to work less abrupt for these young people.

Another important characteristic is the acquisition of a set of skills which, in the long term, provides them with a favourable bargaining position in the labour market and a fair degree of job security. In the short term this acquisition of skills provides a source of satisfaction and interest in their work which is not available to the careerless. In addition, their skilled status means that while they undoubtedly learn to accept the authority of their superiors, the actual performance of their work tasks cannot be dictated in as much detail. Thus while unskilled workers find that jobs which offer them freedom from supervision provide them with more satisfaction than other careerless jobs, these workers always have some such freedom and also a much greater range of activities in which they are involved and in which they can take an interest. Because there are a greater range of areas in which these young workers can develop an interest and derive satisfaction from their work than would be the case among the careerless, they tend to become more involved in it and thus their performance at work becomes an important aspect of the way in which they view themselves. It also means that although these young workers are hoping to achieve greater rewards for their efforts in the short-term future, they may also be obtaining considerable satisfaction from the day-to-day activities involved in the job.

As they progress through this training period their gradual acquisition of new skills and their mastery over increasingly

C

complex tasks provides them with a source of pride and involvement in their work which is lacking for the careerless. It is in this period that their career aspirations normally become crystallized in relation to the structure of opportunities which they learn is available to them. Apart from those who later move into supervisory or higher technical positions it is probably at this period in their career that they experience their greatest involvement in work. Later in their working life their work is less likely to present them with the same challenge and sense of achievement since they will have mastered their skills and thus work becomes more routine. This diminution in the interest which work provides will of course vary considerably from one occupation to another and even within the same occupation. For example, toolmakers probably have more interesting work than secretaries throughout their career. However, some secretaries (and toolmakers) clearly have more interesting work than others.

What all this means for these young people is that they are more likely to see work as playing an important part in their lives than are the careerless, especially at this early stage in their working lives. In their jobs they are once again in positions in which they are working for future rewards and in many cases have to subordinate their desire to maximize their income in the here and now for the sake of greater rewards in the not too distant future. Thus their tendency to direct their behaviour towards more general considerations rather than responding to the demands of the here and now is again reinforced. In their relations with those in authority at work they are learning to accept without question the broad guidelines that define what is permissible, but within these limits they exercise discretion over how they perform their work. The skills that they are acquiring, and the discretion that this gives them in performing their work tasks, are important in that they enable them to think of themselves as getting on in the world and making something of themselves. It means that work is an area of involvement and achievement in a way that it cannot be for those in careerless occupations. By providing them with the opportunity for developing skills that are not only a source of pride and achievement but also promise higher earnings and greater security in later life, work also provides them with a source of support for the development of their identity that is not available for the young workers in careerless occupations. Most of them see themselves as acquiring a trade in order to better themselves, although some do not explicitly see themselves as embarking upon a career. Yet whether they see their intentions in these terms or not, all are setting out to follow a career, albeit one that is relatively short in terms of the number of positions through which they move. Almost all of them have accepted the belief that work should be an area in which one achieves something, and makes something of oneself, and indeed for these young people work provides them with the opportunities and supports to do so.

The differences between these young workers and those in the careerless channel are clearly reflected in their different behaviour in the labour market. Most significantly, these young workers once having entered their first job tend to remain in it at least for the period of their training. Given their outlook, they rarely envisage themselves in any other type of occupation, and indeed very rarely do they seriously consider changing their jobs in the initial stages of their working life. As they are often in the process of learning a fairly complex set of skills, any move from their present job will mean that they will have 'wasted' the time and energy invested in the training period. In addition the variety of tasks on which they are engaged provide an incentive to remain, and in fact if they are going to 'make something of themselves' and acquire the appropriate skills they cannot afford to move without endangering their ambition to be fully qualified. In this they are usually supported not only by their parents but also by their peer group, for to give up their trade will be seen as giving up something which is greatly valued. The longer they spend in their apprenticeship or training the harder it is to move out, not only because some may have signed indentures but because the age restrictions on entry mean that the only alternatives they have if they want to change jobs are those which offer few career chances. The result is that these young people rarely move jobs or even consider this until they have finished their training, at which point considerations of job security and the social status provided by these jobs may further serve to prevent them from changing jobs.[4] The effect of the lengthy period of training and these other factors is to 'lock' the young workers into the specific jobs for which they are trained, and their job mobility is thus restricted to a much narrower range of choice than is the case for those in the careerless channel.

NON-WORK ACTIVITIES

The fact that for these young workers work is an important area of activity and achievement does not prevent them from leading a full and active social life. Indeed, because they have learned to act in accordance with generally accepted adult standards of behaviour at home, and are encouraged at school and work to accept similar standards by those in authority, they 'fit in well' with the youth clubs and other organized activities provided for young people. Because they are used to judging their behaviour by standards similar to those used by the adults that run these activities, they may accept the constraints imposed upon their behaviour by these organizations more easily than the careerless. Whatever the reason, these young workers tend to join such clubs more frequently than the careerless youths, although not all of them join in such organized activities. It should be noted that for these young people their attendance at evening class is likely to reduce the amount of time they have available for non-work activities. This, together with their greater participation in organized activities, means that they are less likely to experience the feelings of boredom with their leisure activities that are sometimes reported by the young people in careerless positions.

We suggest that what all this means is that, while for these young workers their involvement in the 'youth culture' may be important to them, it is not as significant for the development of their identity as it can be for some of the young people in careerless occupations. For these young people, the fact that they are 'making something of themselves' at work means that their leisure activities do not become the sole focus for the development of their identities, nor the only area in which they can achieve the respect of others. The apprentice or trainee is already obtaining this respect from other members of his trade as he acquires the appropriate skills. This does not mean, however, that his leisure activities are not valued as a meaningful source of relationships. What it does mean is that both work and non-work activities and relationships are potentially rewarding. Some of these young people may consider their leisure activities with their friends to be a more meaningful source of relationships to them, in the sense that they have a stronger attachment to the values and interests that they share with their friends than those they share with their fellow workers. Others may consider the interests and values they share with other members of their trade as a more significant part of themselves, but the point is that *both* these areas provide potentially rewarding experiences. While the 'youth culture' may provide them with an interest in clothes, music, and perhaps an alternative set of values to those provided by their parents with regard to such issues as sexual behaviour, it does not provide them with their *only* source of support.

SUMMARY

The young people we have been discussing in this chapter are mainly those from the 'respectable working class'. At home they are brought up in a world which is largely governed by clear and explicit rules, and in which they are encouraged to plan their behaviour by reference to consideration of its consequences in the foreseeable future. In these families the children are likely to acquire values and standards which, while not identical to those transmitted within the school, nevertheless facilitate the children's integration into it. Their moderate success within the school leads them to be allocated to the middle streams of the comprehensives and the upper streams of the secondary-modern schools. There they learn to see themselves as academically inferior to those in either the higher streams or the grammar schools, but still definitely superior to those in the lower streams. They learn to accept the definition of themselves handed down by their teachers as not particularly bright but nevertheless as of some ability and capable of development. This type of self-image is supported by their position within the school which offers them the possibility of moderate academic success. Thus they can expect and are encouraged to work for short-term rewards; which at school means the possibility of some form of minimal educational certification.

Having acquired this type of self-image and orientation to the world, they require that the work they choose should provide them with the possibility of developing their abilities to the full and of 'making something of themselves'. For this reason, and also because they have learnt to orientate themselves towards the short-term future, these young people tend to reject unskilled manual occupations as unsuitable for themselves. They seek entry into those occupations that provide the chance for them to develop their skills and so secure a relatively high level of rewards in the short-term future. They do this in spite of the fact that many unskilled jobs offer them a higher level of earnings initially.

These young people receive confirmation and elaboration of their self-image and orientation to work when they enter what may be termed 'short-term careers'. While these occupations do not provide the extended career ladder characteristic of the 'extended careers', nor anything like the same level of economic rewards, nevertheless they do provide training and security, and the possibility of moving up one or two steps on the career ladder. On entering these occupations the young people are starting a period of training during which they will develop their abilities through the acquisition of the appropriate skills of the trade. This reinforces their image of themselves as capable of development and of 'making something of themselves' through their work. Once again, as in the course of their school career, they will be working for rewards which they can expect to secure in the short-term future, this time in the form of the security and the relatively high earnings that their skills will command. For some of them there may be the vague possibility of moving higher some time later in their career, perhaps to the position of foreman, or its equivalent, but for a substantial proportion the acquisition of the skill is their overriding objective.

A further characteristic of this type of occupation is that it provides substantial scope for the people who enter it to derive intrinsic satisfaction from their work. It means that in the course of their work the young workers can develop a sense of pride in the skills they acquire as well as an interest in the practical problems which their work presents. It means that in the short term at least their work is a source of personal achievement. However, once they have qualified, most of them are no longer involved in an attempt to 'get on' and so their work will not demand the subordination of their other interests to work as will be the case for those young people following extended careers.

Notes

1   Many of these occupations are to be found in the more modern industries in the expanding sector of the economy. As we pointed out in Chapter 2, such industries are mainly located in the southern part of England.

2   S. Coopersmith, *The Antecedents of Self-Esteem*, San Francisco and London: W. H. Freeman, 1967, discusses the importance of clear rules in the family and how they facilitate freedom and autonomy for the children.

3   Some technical occupations provide the chance of career movement into managerial positions, although such opportunities are minimal and depend on the acquisition of high level educational qualifications.

4   The end of training often coincides with marriage for these young workers, and it is marriage which often serves to focus questions about their work future. For the young men there may be a push towards semi-skilled work which provides immediately higher levels of income which have to be weighed against the greater security and possibly long-term higher income of their trade. For the young women this is often the point at which they leave the labour market, having acquired a skill which will allow them to return to work after raising a family.

5. Extended Careers

The types of occupations entered by the young people we discuss in this chapter are some of those which provide the possibility of an extended career. There are two main types of entry pattern into occupations which provide extended careers, each of which is related to differences between such occupations. One group consist of the 'early' school-leavers who tend to enter managerial, administrative and certain commercial occupations. This group of young people are to a certain extent the pupils who either do not see themselves as having the ability to continue on beyond 'Ordinary' or 'Advanced' level, or who wish to leave immediately they have obtained the appropriate qualifications for entry to an extended career. Not surprisingly they contain a higher proportion of children from working-class families than will be found among the largely middle-class group who continued on into higher education. (These upwardly mobile working-class children will be most likely to come from the type of family situation described in Chapter 4.) This group, then, is much more varied in social background than the groups considered in Chapters 3 and 4. However, in order to make our discussion as clear as possible we shall restrict ourselves to considering the main characteristics of children from middle-class families, since they provide the largest group entering this type of occupation.

The second group entering extended careers are those who continue on to some form of full-time higher education before entering work, and for these reasons we do not consider them in this book. These tend to enter the 'higher' professions and to enter managerial and administrative positions at a higher level.

In relation to the other types of families we have studied, middle-class families command considerably greater monetary resources. It is not just the size of the resources which is important, but also that they progressively increase for the greater part of the working life. These families are thus normally certain that their standard of living will improve from year to year for a considerable period of time. This fact, plus the general security of their jobs, makes the situation facing members of these families very different from that facing the members of working-class families. It means that the management of the household finances raises few serious day-to-day problems of the type facing the working classes, for the resources at the command of the parents are easily sufficient to cover expenses. In addition, with the help of various commercial agencies such as the banks, these can be taken out of the hands of the parents and so become a matter of routine commercial business. Further, such families are 'good credit risks' and are able to secure short-term loans and overdrafts to tide them over periods of financial difficulty. Another consequence of these greater resources is that the wife can frequently be relieved of the more routine work of the household either through the acquisition of a wide range of household appliances or through the employment of domestic help. Finally, the level and dependability of income is such that it allows these families to live in larger and 'better' houses where there is more space for all members of the family (e.g. a room for each child).

Although the income which work provides is obviously of central importance, as is the case with the working-class families, other aspects of work also have an important influence on family life. In contrast to workers in the other channels the successful performance of most middle-class jobs requires the mastery of inter-personal skills since much of the work depends upon a complex system of co-operation and co-ordination of workers. Whereas in the working-class occupations tasks are more clearly defined by the employing organization and the co-operation and co-ordination of workers is imposed from above, in these occupations tasks cannot be as clearly defined, nor can the relationships between workers be as simply controlled. Indeed they are often in positions where they exercise considerable control over their work activities and many of them will hold positions of authority over other people.

Another aspect of the middle-class work situation is the centrality of the husband's career. This tends to determine the level at which they currently live, the area where they reside and the people they currently mix with. The fact that the husband's success or failure within his career can make significant differences to the status of the family and the resources at its disposal is usually sufficient to maintain his dominance within the family. Such dominance is also found in the working-class families we have discussed, and for them also the general status of the family and its style of life is dependent on the husband's occupation. In middle-class families, however, the impact of the husband's occupation is more direct and all-pervasive. It does not merely provide the basis for family life via the provision of income and prestige, but it actively affects the whole range of family activities and relationships. It means, for example, that other members of the family may have to be prepared to sacrifice their present friendships if progress in the husband's career demands a change of residence to a new locality. It also means that given the possibility of greater rewards for the husband in the future as he progresses in his career, the emphasis in the family is on long-term planning and ensuring that the plans materialize, even if this means the subordination of satisfactions in the here and now. One significant feature of such behaviour is the planning of children both in timing and numbers, often resulting in families that are smaller than working-class families.

The middle class also differ significantly from the working classes with regard to the way they relate to the labour market and the community. Whereas the lower working class are orientated to the local labour market and also to the local community, often sharing non-work activities with others in the local community, the situation with the middle class is very different. While there is a section of the middle class that tends to participate in the local community activities, namely that part of the middle class with local roots such as family businesses, they do so through participating in local politics and in positions of social leadership. There is, however, another part of the middle class that is orientated to the national community in that they have few local ties and their friendship networks tend to expand well beyond the geographical limitations of the local community. For both of these groups, but particularly for the latter, their work and leisure activities involve them in a series of independent, non-overlapping groups in which the participants have shared experiences over a relatively narrow range.

These features of work and non-work activities influence family life in a number of ways. While their economic position enables them to plan ahead in a way similar to that discussed in the previous chapter, such planning can be over a much longer range due to the larger income. As with the short-term career families, planning extends to family leisure activities and can be used as a means of controlling the children's behaviour (as we have shown in Chapter 4). Another important way in which income affects the children is that they are brought up in families in which considerable resources can be devoted to providing a suitable environment for the children in which they can learn to explore the world. In a material sense the parents can and do provide the right kind of 'educational' toys and often enrol their children in such pre-school organizations as play groups and nursery schools. Thus from an early age these children have access to a variety of experiences that may not be available to working-class children.

Related to these material differences are differences in the quality of the relationships between parents and children. The mother, because she has fewer day-to-day problems to worry about, fewer children to care for, and less time taken up with routine domestic chores, has more time and energy to devote to the children. Further, where the children are sent to play groups or nursery schools or are looked after for part of the day by nannies, the emotional demands made by them upon their mothers are less continuous and demanding. What all this means is that parent-child contacts within these families have a different character to those described in the previous chapters. In these families children are much more likely to be responded to in terms of their unique individual characteristics. For example, within this type of family, age and sex differences are not as important as they are in the working class. What is emphasized in the children's relationships with their parents is not only the distinctiveness of their sex role or the position they occupy as a child within the family, but also their specific characteristics as individuals in their own right. They are encouraged to participate in discussions with their parents and are not as frequently excluded or told to 'shut up' because they are children. Similarly, while their sexual identity is made clear, the boundaries that separate behaviour that is appropriate for girls from that appropriate for boys are far more blurred than they are in working-class families. For girls, however, the expectations regarding their behaviour are more clearly tied to their sex, and they are given less freedom of action than is the case with boys. This is a general feature of all types of families in our society;[1] however, it is in middle-class families that girls are given most freedom. The very language used by the parents reflects this type of openness in family relationships, emphasizing as it does the uniqueness of the children's experience and encouraging them to make explicit the reasons for their actions and requests.

This type of relationship is clearly tied up with the subordination of the immediate rewards of behaviour to considerations of longer-term consequences and is reinforced by the manner in which authority is exercised with the family. Both husband and wife in their non-family life operate in a series of situations where they constantly have to make explicit the bases of their actions and hence also tend to do so in their relations with their children. Broad guidelines are laid down for the children but the reasoning behind them is made explicit, both in terms of general considerations governing behaviour and in terms of the individual needs of the parents and children. While the persistent transgression of parental guidelines will be punished systematically, within them the children are encouraged to exercise their initiative and to question the basis of relationships they enter into. The children not only learn the general social conventions governing behaviour but also learn that they should shape their behaviour within the limits of these conventions, and that they should take into consideration the needs of others. An example will clarify the difference between this style of social control and the less 'person-oriented' style found in other types of family. In the latter type of family children are told to 'kiss Grandad goodbye' either with no explanation at all, or the 'explanation' that this is what is expected of children. In middle-class families children are given the further information that they should 'kiss Grandad good-bye' because, although they may not like doing so, it is the kind of thing good children do *because it pleases Grandad.* We are not saying that such consideration of the needs of others is absent in working-class families. The important point is that it is made explicit to the children in middle-class families, and they are encouraged to learn to relate to others in terms of their individual needs and characteristics, and not simply in terms of clearly apparent indicators such as age and sex.[2] Clearly this type of explication is only possible where parents have the time and energy to explain the often complex under-lying aspects of social behaviour, and is more frequently avail-able in middle-class families due in part to their greater material resources.

The effect of the children's experience in these relationships is that they learn to internalize certain general principles which guide their behaviour. However, while they guide their behaviour in terms of these principles they can apply them flexibly to take account of the exigencies of the immediate situation. We suggest that this style of behaviour is different from that transmitted and internalized in short-term career families where rules are more dogmatic and inflexible. For these children there is a large area where they are encouraged to exercise their initiative in their relationships with others. They learn to relate to others not so much in terms of immediate rewards and consequences but primarily in terms of the long-term rewards that can be achieved. It is this concern with the long-term rewards that is one of the most distinctive features of the way in which they come to view the world. Another im-portant consequence is that they come to see themselves as capable of having a considerable effect on their world and to be able to plan their behaviour over a long period of time to achieve such desired effects. This is an important element in the development of the pattern of *deferred gratifications* which social scientists have identified as an important distinguishing charac-

teristic of the middle class. Unless one is confident of being
able to realise long-term goals there is no incentive to defer
immediate rewards.

Another important element which clearly supports this style
of family relationship is the educational background of the
parents. In these families either one or both parents are likely
to have both the knowledge and the social skills that enable
them to make the most of the 'system'. That is, they know
where and how to acquire relevant information about such
things as schooling, finance and the like. They have a clear
idea of what is demanded of their children if they are to get on
well at school and make more use of pre-school training than
other parents. This ensures that their children are not only
prepared for school when they officially start but also that they
are educationally advanced from the beginning. The parents
know what subjects it is important for their children to do well
in, and they not only know the significance of the decisions that
teachers take about streaming but are more prepared to take
action to ensure that the outcomes are in accord with their wish
for the child. Finally, they are not intimidated by the authority
of the teachers and can speak to them 'on their own level'.

SCHOOL EXPERIENCE

Largely because of their family background children from
middle-class families are likely to experience little difficulty in
fitting in at school. The social background of their teachers is
likely to be similar to that of their parents and, indeed, their
attempts to make a career are similar to the career struggles
which the parents are involved in. If we look at specific areas
more closely then it is clear that unlike the young pupils from a
working-class background, these young pupils will find few
areas where there is any clash between their values, their way
of relating to others, their interests, and those of their teachers.
They also experience little difficulty with the formal language
used by their teachers and in their textbooks, and are hardly
likely to encounter the problem often voiced by pupils in the
lower streams that 'half the time I couldn't understand what
the teachers were talking about', at least not as a persistent

problem. Of course in some lessons and with some teachers they are likely to experience difficulties in understanding but this is unlikely to be a permanent feature of their school life. It is not simply that they can understand the language which is used, but also that they have a better appreciation of what they are trying to do since their home experience has taught them to look for general principles as well as immediately apparent features of behaviour.

Their appreciation of the aims of school derives from a set of values which is shared by the teachers, children and parents. School is seen not simply as a place where certain minimal skills are obtained but as also concerned with the development of 'potential' and the furthering of special abilities and interests. Parents and teachers in particular are likely to view education as an attempt to develop various facets of the children's personalities. Whereas the working-class children, with their 'pragmatic' view of education, are unlikely to find subjects such as music or history relevant, for these children such subjects are likely to be seen as just as important as 'more practical' subjects because of their intrinsic interest. In any case a good performance in these subjects is just as important from a utilitarian point of view as another 'Ordinary' or 'Advanced' level pass.

Given the similarity between their home backgrounds and their experience of school, there is little wonder that middle-class children tend to perform well at school. The result is that they are usually placed in the higher streams of the comprehensives and, where they still exist, in the grammar schools. Here they are once again, as at home, given every support for the development of their interests and abilities. They tend to be provided with the most qualified teachers, they tend to have a higher teacher-pupil ratio, and in addition are offered the highest rewards and resources the school can provide, thus maximizing their likely success in the external school examinations. Their allocation to the higher streams not only virtually guarantees their access to occupations providing an extended career, but has an important effect on their view of themselves and their future. The system of beliefs that are used to justify streaming provides them with confirmation of their image of themselves as capable of intellectual development, for teachers tend to see them as 'the cream of their age group' and as possessing superior abilities to the young people in the lower streams. Their teachers also expect them to do well at school and to enter 'good' and 'interesting' occupations where their abilities will not be 'wasted'. Thus these young pupils are surrounded by parents and teachers who define them as capable of getting on and making something of themselves.

The allocation of upwardly mobile working-class children to the upper streams of the state school system has equally profound effects on them and their parents. For these children such allocation is a clear indication of their superiority and may well serve to alter the ways in which they view themselves and their future prospects. In this respect the grammar school not only results in the child 'raising' its occupational aspirations but also modifies the child's values and attitudes in such a way as to contribute towards its successful adaptation to the demands of middle-class occupations. There is some scattered evidence to suggest that parental attitudes towards the child are also affected. It seems that the favourable evaluation of the child by the school and the transmission of this evaluation to the working-class family, and in particular to the mother, alters the family's attitudes and actions so as to discriminate in favour of the 'brighter' child by supporting and encouraging the child in its school work. For those working-class children attending secondary modern schools but with the same 'objective' intellectual ability as the 11-plus successes, school has no such effect. One of the effects of the abolition of the 11-plus and the introduction of 'open' comprehensives has been to reduce the visibility (and importance) of such indicators of 'academic potential' to the parents and their children. There is some evidence to suggest that in this situation parental attitudes play a more significant part in determining the level at which their children enter the labour market than is the case under a system of streaming. The paradox is that in many cases these attitudes are themselves based on academic indicators of the child's performance.

The pattern of deferred gratification is reinforced by their school experiences for both middle-class and upwardly mobile working-class children. While they undoubtedly derive considerable satisfaction from the development of their interests and skills in the course of their day-to-day lessons, they are primarily working for the longer-term rewards that successful performance at 'Ordinary' and 'Advanced' level bring. For them their present activities are primarily experienced as a preparation for the future. Thus they consider the work and activities that they are engaged in at school not only in terms of their immediate rewards and satisfactions but also in terms of their long-term benefits.

The school also affects the way these young people view work, and for the middle-class children reinforces the general values about work and conduct which are held by the children's parents. Unlike those destined for a short-term career, who are interested in the 'practical subjects', these young pupils tend to be directed away from them towards the more 'academic' subjects. It is their skills in the manipulation of symbols that are developed rather than their skills in the manipulation of objects, which in the context of the more academic streams are frequently devalued, either directly or by implication. It is thus not surprising that these young people come to regard manual occupations as 'beneath them'. The emphasis placed on loyalty to the school, initiative, self-discipline, and hard work as necessary for ensuring personal advancement in life not only reinforces what the young pupils learn at home from their parents, but also prepares them for the competitive struggle for advancement which they will face at work. Loyalty to the school is valued and rewarded by appointment to positions of responsibility within the school (such as prefect) in much the same way as their future loyalty to their employers will be rewarded by promotion within the organization. Similarly the 'virtue' of hard work is rewarded at school by praise and acclaim from the teachers after successful examination performance, as well as by the direct awarding of prizes and honours. Self-discipline and initiative are similarly rewarded. Thus these values (which as we have seen are largely irrelevant to young workers entering careerless occupations) come to occupy a central place in the way these young people act towards the world.

It almost goes without saying that these young people do not experience their relationship with the school as one of conflict in the way in which those destined for careerless occupations do. This is not to say that specific individuals do not find aspects of their school life annoying, e.g. games or homework, but as a group these young pupils tend to experience their time at school as fairly interesting and unproblematic. In particular, and by contrast to the careerless, they experience few problems with the authority system of the school, as they share similar values to their teachers. The teachers experience relatively few difficulties with these children, partly due to the various forms of reward and praise which they can offer them for the successful performance of their school tasks. Their relationships with their teachers encourage them, as did their relationships with their parents, to take over adult standards as their own. Indeed as their parents' and teachers' standards are likely to be similar the young pupils rapidly learn to control their own behaviour in accordance with such standards and, within the limits permitted by them, to exercise initiative. Should they fail to abide by the expected patterns of behaviour then the teachers have the very powerful sanction of demotion to a lower stream. Through demotion the teacher can effectively reduce the chances of the young people obtaining the kind of occupation which they believe they are worthy of. With this combination of external sanction and internal control, behaviour at school does not appear to be a problem to the teacher.

ENTRY INTO WORK

Given their integration into the school and general enjoyment of school life, why is it that these young people leave school 'early' rather than continue at school? Probably the most important reason is because of their failure to achieve the requisite level of performance in 'Ordinary' level or similar examinations which prevents them continuing on to higher education. At the same time there are those who although achieving the requisite level nevertheless feel they have reached their educational limit. A second important reason, and one which is probably more relevant for the upwardly mobile working-class children, is limited financial resources of the families. A third factor which is obviously relevant in some cases, again more commonly for the working-class children, is tension with the school. While most children may be integrated into the school in the sense that they accept the values transmitted and are interested in the subjects, they may find their subordinate position in the school irksome, particularly if they have friends who are working, and so wish to leave. There will also be those who have had enough of formal education, and feel that they wish to do something 'practical' with their lives. Finally, there are those who have carefully considered their future career and have decided that it is in their best interest to enter on-the-job training schemes at the earliest opportunity, e.g. entering into articles or sandwich courses.

The strategies adopted by these school-leavers in finding their first jobs reflect the fairly extensive investment they have made in their education. They have been working towards their educational qualifications for a number of years and want to make the most of these qualifications. They are usually very clear about the jobs which will *not* allow them to do this and have learnt to dismiss manual work as unsuitable. They are, however, usually unclear as to the exact nature of their future work although they are all certain that it must have 'prospects'.[3] What is meant by 'prospects' varies from one young person to another in much the same way as the perceived advantages of having a trade varies from one apprentice to another. The common element is that the rewards to which they refer can only be obtained in the long term. In some cases the prospects are the long-term security and pensions associated with the jobs, in others they are the chances of holding positions of responsibility, and for yet others the prospects are seen as the chance for advancement, not just in the next few years, but throughout the major part of their working life. Given their background it is hardly surprising that these young people should subordinate their concern for immediate rewards or short-term rewards for the greater rewards which they think can be obtained in the long run from these occupations. Thus they are quite happy to accept jobs with relatively low starting salaries because of their perceived long-term prospects, including the eventually higher salaries that are possible. This is not to say that 'immediate' considerations are unimportant, for they will often determine the choice made between different long-term career occupations, in much the same way that they operate for those entering short-term careers.

The type of job which these young people are aiming for also affects the strategies they use. We have already said that they may be unclear as to their 'choice' of work. This lack of clarity is partly a result of the much broader range of possible jobs which they are faced with when compared to those school-leavers entering other occupational channels. Further, they are seeking entry into occupations which have a variety of different entrance requirements. These occupations are also more differentiated from each other with respect to the eventual levels and types of reward which they offer to successful workers than is the case with occupations in the other channels we have discussed. Some, such as solicitors and chartered accountants, have a relatively short career ladder in comparison to others, although informally there may be a number of steps beyond the period of formal training. By comparison, many careers in administration tend to have a much greater number of formally recognized steps. Again, in comparison to such formally defined career hierarchies, there are other careers in which the probable pattern of movement and eventual possible level of success is hard for the school-leaver to assess. For example, while the school-leaver may 'know' that a job in banking offers a 50 per cent chance (for males) of becoming a manager, it may be much less clear what his future prospects are in an industrial organization, although it may be clear that success in this context brings much greater rewards in terms of salary and associated 'perks' than in banking. A final point is that if these young people are to realize their job requirements they must often look beyond the local labour market. Thus, faced with a bewildering variety of different occupations each with its own separate entrance requirements and offering different prospects, these prospective young workers are more likely to use the formal channels of information and to rely more on the knowledge of careers specialists and that which can be found in specialist publications than on the more informal channels.

The short-term career perspective is clearly not inconsistent with entry into extended careers, and indeed we suspect that a number of young people holding such an orientation do in fact enter such careers without realizing the long-term opportunities open to them. Such people will include not only the working-class children who were always successful at school but also those who achieve unexpected success in their final school examinations as a result of which they decide to enter more prestigious 'middle-class' occupations.

WORK EXPERIENCE

It seems that these young people do not look forward to their entry into work in quite the same way as other school-leavers, partly because of their relatively high integration into their schools. Unlike the careerless they are not longing for their 'release' from school, but view leaving school as a logical step which has to be made. The transition from school to work is eased by many similarities between their work situation (particularly for those who enter office jobs) and that of school. One element of this is that for most of them there is continuity in their education either in the form of 'on-the-job' instruction or by way of day release and night school courses connected with their work. The major difference, and the primary advantages, of their experience of work in comparison to that of school is the feeling of greater freedom and responsibility that work gives. Even here, however, there is not a sharp contrast (as is the case with the careerless, and to a lesser extent those entering short-term careers) for at school, and particularly in the sixth forms, they are given some control over the way in which they do their work.

The lengthy period of training characteristic of these occupations has similar consequences for these young workers to those which affect the short-term career worker. That is, it provides a source of interest and involvement in work; security resulting from the acquisition of expertise; and it serves to make job changing difficult in the early stages of work. The main differences are to be found in the longer period of training and the type of skills acquired. These careers involve the acquisition of

85

more than a fixed set of skills which are then utilized in various situations, and the process of learning is more continuous, and often involves acquiring new skills at each stage of the career. Further, these skills tend to be less task-specific and therefore facilitate movement between occupations later in the career because of their applicability to a wide range of tasks. Finally, the acquisition of these theoretical and practical skills will often take anything up to ten years.

This process of continually acquiring new and changing skills requires elaboration as it has a number of important consequences. In the early stages of their careers these young workers will be concerned with acquiring the basic skills and symbols on which their claim to professional and technical competence is based. As they progress, it will become increasingly important for them to acquire skills of an inter-personal kind. Unlike the skilled workers who remain in the same position in relation to other groups that comprise the organization within which they work, these young workers can expect to move through a series of different organizationally defined positions in the course of their careers. At each stage they will have to learn to relate to the other groups that comprise the organization in a different way, and they can expect to move from subordinate positions to positions of some authority during the course of their working life. Their relationships with others thus may always involve more general long-term considerations as well as those related to the immediate situation, because their advancement will depend to a certain extent upon how well they can handle such relationships. For someone from a middle-class background this may not be too difficult to cope with, for in their family situation they will have learned to question the basis of relationships and to manipulate them, and to subordinate immediate rewards to more general considerations. For someone from a working-class background who has learnt to exercise discretion only within the confines of unquestioned or absolute rules, this will be more difficult. For these young workers success at work will not only lead to the development of their 'practical' skills, it will often also lead to the development of certain skills in relating to people. The result is that as their confidence in handling situations increases their self-esteem is likely to be enhanced at each successfully completed stage of their career. In this way, then, their occupation plays an important part in the development of their identity.

Probably the most important characteristic of these occupations is the uncertainty that surrounds the final 'career level' that will be reached by those who enter them. This uncertainty is due in part to the hierarchical ordering of the positions that comprise the occupation, for there are a greater number of positions at the bottom than at the top so that not all who start can reach the top. While the rewards that these young workers seek are potentially high both in terms of the material benefits and the achievement of securing membership of high status professional or occupational groups, there is great uncertainty as to which level of these rewards they will eventually receive. By contrast those who are entering careerless jobs or those offering a short-term career know with some certainty what their future at work will be. We are not suggesting that this uncertainty is immediately problematic for these young workers (although it may become so in later years), but it has a number of important consequences. First, the lengthy period of training is often seen as a way of minimizing this uncertainty by providing the formal skills and training necessary for future career advancement. Such training in itself, however, is quickly recognized to be insufficient to secure advancement and the young workers become aware of the importance of interpersonal skills, such as 'the ability to get on with other people'. In many occupations the criteria used for deciding who will be promoted are not always clearly defined, and neither are the jobs. In such situations the young workers have to search for cues as to what is appropriate behaviour for someone in their position, but in the absence of *clear* guidelines by which they can assess how well or badly they are performing. One of the few ways they can assure themselves they are succeeding is to create a 'name' for themselves, and it is often left to them to make what they can out of their positions. The often intense competition for promotion together with the lack of clear guidelines are the main elements generating uncertainty about their future at work. This is the case even in organizations where

87

educational qualifications are used as criteria for promotion. This uncertainty and the anxiety it creates becomes an increasingly important feature of their lives as they become older.

The uncertainty of the outcome of their struggle for advancement interacts with the lengthy period of training to generate higher levels of involvement in their work for these young people than for those in other occupations. As we have seen, the process of learning is extended over a considerable period of time, during the course of which the young worker is continually meeting new problems. In this sense work has the potential for continuously generating interest on the part of those who move from one rung to the next on the career ladder. While on the one hand work provides this opportunity for the young people to become involved in the tasks, on the other hand the uncertainty of the outcome of the 'promotion race' creates pressures on them to subordinate their other interests to work. In many cases they may have to be prepared to move away from their present circle of friends and their local community and work in another town if promotion entails this. They will have to be prepared to accept that work may involve the sacrifice of some of their leisure time if promotion is to be achieved, and they may have to organize their leisure activities so that they are complementary to their work. Such sacrifices are particularly evident in the early stages of work when their engagement in further education and the perceived importance of 'doing the right things' in the 'right' places restrict their leisure activities.

For these young workers, especially the boys, leisure activities are often seen as having to take second place to work. In this they are supported by parents, older colleagues at work, and their friends who are usually in similar positions. This is in contrast to young workers following short-term careers who, while they often regard work and leisure as of equal value, seem to make a more rigid separation between the two.

Once again we find that their occupation is more salient for the young men than young women, although this situation appears to be changing slowly. For young women in this channel their occupations play a much more important and significant role in their lives than is the case with young women in the lower channels. It is in this channel that the choice between a successful work career and starting a family is more problematic. We should add that women are often denied career advancement because it is assumed that work is of secondary importance to them, even if this is not the case. In those cases where the choice is genuinely problematic the lack of prospects at work may be the factor deciding them to subordinate their work to the more traditional female role of housewife and mother. In this way a 'self-fulfilling prophecy' is perpetuated.

For these young workers, as with the other groups we have discussed, their experience of work confirms the ways of looking at their world which they developed in the home and school. In particular they are confirmed in their acceptance of the beliefs transmitted by the media and their teachers that everyone should make a career, and that to progress from positions of low prestige, income, and authority to positions of higher income, prestige and authority is an indication of individual worth. To these young people such ambition is something everyone ought to have and the lack of it is seen as a sign of inadequacy. To improve oneself through success in a competitive struggle for advancement at work is seen as a universal characteristic of life. In this way they can speak of *'everyone's* ambition to get to the top', since for them it is obvious that anyone at work would want to get on. As we have seen, however, this is *not* the fact for all young people, for some have little or no chance of moving up one step, let alone getting to the 'top'. The value attached to ambition and getting on does make sense to these young people, however, and sustains them in their continuous struggle for advancement.

NON-WORK ACTIVITIES

The first point to be noted about the non-work activities of this group of young people is that for many of them a substantial proportion of their non-work time will be taken up by work-related activities such as night school or preparation for professional examinations. By contrast to those young people we have already discussed, this group spends a large proportion of its leisure time in activities organized by clubs or associations. In particular it is in this group that membership of special interest groups such as archery clubs or church discussion groups is highest. They are also the group which seems to experience the least boredom in their leisure time activities. It is clear that for the vast majority of them the so called 'youth culture' is not a central focus of their activities as it is for some of the other young workers.[4] While it is something they participate in, the world of youth culture can never provide the kind of rewards which they eventually anticipate from their world of work. Indeed, for many of them their leisure activities in general cannot hold out the promise of satisfaction and rewards similar to those they expect from work. Their work thus becomes of central interest, in the sense that they subordinate their other activities to it and start to use their success at work as a means of measuring their personal worth.

SUMMARY

The young people we have discussed are primarily those who are from middle-class families or who have been upwardly mobile from a working-class background. They are the children who have moved through the older type of grammar school or the higher streams in the comprehensives. For these young people there is likely to be a good 'fit' between the culture of the family and that of the school and so the children are likely to be aware of the relationship between successful school performance and their later entry into a 'good' career. The image they acquire of themselves within the family as clever and capable of making a success of themselves is reinforced by their allocation to the higher streams of the schools. There they learn to see themselves in the same way as their teachers and others see them, i.e. as 'bright', of superior ability, and capable of considerable self-development. Throughout their school life they are taught that loyalty, self-discipline and hard work are essential for success in the competitive struggle for advancement they are involved in at school and will be involved in in their future career. In school they are encouraged, as they are at home, to focus on the long-term rewards and benefits that their present efforts can bring. For them the present is experienced as a preparation for the long-term future, for they are encouraged to forego certain forms of immediate gratification and to seek out the long-term rewards that the development of their potential will bring. Predictably they aim to enter those occupations that offer them the chance of developing their abilities and from which in the long term they can obtain the greatest rewards. For them their success in competition with others at school has been a measure of their personal worth and they expect to obtain further confirmation of their personal worth as a result of their success in the competitive struggle for advancement they will face at work.

Most of these young people are successful in gaining entry to occupations that provide them with the chance of fairly continuous advancement throughout the greater part of their working life. These occupations we have described as providing *extended careers*. They provide the highest and most secure incomes as a reward for those who are successful in climbing the career ladder. Once in such occupations the young persons' experience of work confirms and elaborates their self-images and orientations to work in a number of ways. The fact that such occupations provide a relatively long career ladder means that the young people who enter them are once again working, as they were at school, for long-term rewards. Their image of themselves as bright and capable of development is reinforced in such situations, for once again they are embarking on a long period of learning. Moreover in some of these occupations they can expect to be developing their potential skills over the greater part of their working life, as they may be required to master new skills at each major stage in their occupational career. For them the present is again experienced as a preparation for the future. The images they have of themselves are not shaped only by their present occupational activities but also by their potential achievements. Once again they are involved in a competitive struggle for advancement, this time within a career in which the fruits of success, in terms of the salary they can eventually obtain and the authority and prestige they can command, are substantially greater than those available to other young people. However, for them to be certain of achieving this success they will have to concentrate their efforts and subordinate their other interests to their work.

The experience these young people have of work tends to confirm the beliefs transmitted by their parents, teachers and the media that a career of this sort is something to be highly valued and well worth striving for. They now see themselves with the chance of securing substantial economic rewards and a very high standard of living if they are successful in climbing the career ladder. The fact that they are already successful in entering this type of occupation tends to support the image they hold of themselves as possessing superior abilities to other young people. The possibility of substantial rewards in the future now reinforces those qualities such as hard work, self-discipline and devotion to duty which they were taught at school would ensure such success. The possibility of securing such substantial rewards means that work remains of central importance to these young people, and their success in it is seen as an important measure of their personal worth.

Notes

1 For a more detailed discussion of the class differences in the socialization of women see A. Oakley, *The Sociology of Housework*, London: Martin Robertson 1974.

2 This example is drawn directly from the work of B. Bernstein, on whom we have drawn in our discussions of parent-child relationships in all three chapters. See B. Bernstein (ed.), *Class, Codes and Control*, Vols. I and II, London: Routledge and Kegan Paul, 1972 and 1973.

3 As we shall show, because of the difficulties they face in making an informed choice, these school-leavers may find themselves in jobs which do not fulfil their career expectations. We suggest, however, that due to the indeterminacy of career structures in these types of occupation, it is more normally the case that it is only relatively late in their working lives that such realizations occur. As this latter case is clearly beyond the focus of the present book we do no more than mention it. Its implication for the present work is that this group of young workers is unproblematic mainly because it takes longer for the problems of work to become apparent, whereas for the other young workers discussed the problems posed by work become more immediately apparent.

4 This group of young people should not be confused with those continuing on to full-time higher education. This latter group is not subject

to the conservative constraints imposed upon the present group in its struggle for acceptance and success at work. Not only do those in higher education have more time to devote to leisure activities of a 'cultural' nature, but they are also encouraged to do so. The more 'radical' section of the so-called youth culture seems to be based upon them. See for example, Frank Musgrove, *Ecstasy and Holiness: Counter-Culture and the Open Society*, London: Methuen 1974.

6. Adjustment to Work

The picture which we have drawn in the preceding three chapters presents a deliberately simplified and rather static picture of what is in fact a series of dynamic relationships. As the young people move through the various positions they occupy at school and later at work, so the changing relationships entered into in these situations feed back and affect the relationships within the family. For example, the young person's progression through school serves as a visible indicator of increasing maturity and independence. In the case of those young people who experience a basic continuity between home, school and work, entry into work is merely another step in a series of continual adjustments within their families to meet their emergent adult status. The evidence shows that a minimum of 40 per cent of school-leavers enter the same occupational channel as their parents. While this does not mean that they were necessarily in the corresponding educational channel it does indicate that they are unlikely to experience any severe conflicts between the perspective acquired at home and that appropriate to their work situation.

There will, of course, be cases where there is no such continuity. However, most of the young workers who are mobile are so only over a short distance and in fact most of them move into an occupational channel adjacent to that of their parents. (This is illustrated in Diagram 1.) In such cases the allocation of the children to a lower or higher stream than that initially 'expected' by their parents may serve as an early signal to the parents that their child is destined for an occupation that is slightly higher or lower on the social scale than their own. When the family accepts the definitions of the children and their work

94

future which are transmitted within the school, while the children may experience some problems at school they are unlikely to do so at work. In such cases the school is most clearly fulfilling its function of preparation and placement of young people in future occupations. The more acute problems are likely to be experienced where the children and their parents do not accept the implications of the school's definition of the child.

Let us look more closely at this situation where there is incongruity between school and family. If we look first at the case where the school defines the child as bright, this will only apply in the context of this discussion to the children from working-class families. ('Bright' children from middle-class families continue within the educational system, entering the labour market much later in life.) Even within the context of the working classes there is a significant difference as to whether the bright child comes from a family in which the short-term career or careerless perspective is transmitted. In the first case, allocation into the upper streams may well be welcomed by parents and children, resulting in a redefinition within the context of the family of the children's abilities and of the kind of occupation for which they are destined. While this may create tension in the family as its members adjust to the new set of relationships with which the child is involved, they may nevertheless attempt to provide some support for the child in its attempt to perform well at school. In the more 'traditional' working-class communities a high level of success at school may be associated with strain between the 'bright' pupil and his local friends.

The problems encountered by 'bright' working-class children will be more severe for those coming from 'careerless' families for it is in these cases that the differences between home and school are most likely to create acute problems of 'adjustment'. If the children accept the school's definition of their abilities and adopt the behavioural standards transmitted by their teachers, then this is likely to disrupt fundamentally relationships within the family, and in particular the ways in which parents attempt to relate to their children. On the other hand, if they continue to adhere to the perspectives transmitted in the home, then this will bring them into direct conflict with their teachers. A frequent way of resolving this is for the young people to reject one or the other set of values, usually by rejecting those of the school and leaving early, perhaps entering work offering a short-term career. If the children should accept the beliefs and values transmitted by the school, then the transformation of their identity and the ways in which they relate to others may cause them to reject their family of origin.

Those families with children who are allocated to lower positions at school than was expected face similar problems. For children from a family which transmits a short-term career perspective the problem may not be too acute, especially if the redefinition of their ability that takes place at school is accepted by the family which nevertheless continues to give them support. Similarly those young people from families that transmit a long-term career perspective, and who enter the middle levels of the state school system, will not experience acute problems if the parents support and accept the change implied. It is in the more extreme cases of downward mobility that the young people experience more acute problems, and it is in these cases that parents and children will have the greatest difficulty in accepting the definitions of the child and its future which are being transmitted at school.

We do not mean by this discussion to imply that parents and teachers should encourage children to discard attitudes and aspirations acquired within the family if this is incongruent with the situation they face at school. There are a number of strategies that parents can adopt to ensure that their children enter 'suitable' employment. Where the signal from the school comes through to middle-class parents early in the child's school life then they may, if they have the resources, transfer the child to the private sector of the educational system in order to ensure that it eventually enters a middle-class career. In other cases parents are able to ensure that their son has access to a middle-class career when his schooling is completed by calling upon social and family networks. What this may mean is that while such young people will experience considerable problems in the course of their schooling this is considered a worthwhile price to pay for their eventual entry to a 'good' job. Similarly many working-class parents refuse to accept that a bad performance at school may keep their son from entering a job offering a short-term career, and so they attempt to combat the effect that their son's low position at school has on his self-image and orientation to others, and use their knowledge and connections in the local labour market to gain his entry into an occupation providing a short-term career. We have deliberately restricted this discussion to sons because parents are more likely to accept the school's definition of their daughters, and less likely to see this as crucial for their future well-being, which is often seen as largely dependent on making the 'right' marriage.

While the interrelationships between the children's experiences at home and school are one important source of potential problems, there are obviously others. Sources of conflict and tension inhere in almost all inter-personal relationships and learning to cope with them is part of the process of growing up; as one would expect, in many cases these adjustments often involve considerable strains and tensions within the family. However, only in the more extreme cases where the conflicts are particularly acute will they be experienced as constituting major problems for the young people concerned. The central theme of this process is the changing patterns of dependency between children and their parents which involve a shift towards increasingly egalitarian relationships within the family, although this is often not explicitly recognized by the parents. These changes within the family are closely related to changes in other areas. Hence many of the problems faced at this stage are focused not simply on the changing status of the young people within their families but also on changing relationships in other contexts.

One area of particular importance relates to the changing relationships between the sexes. It is during the early years of work that the problems of negotiating sexual relationships and particularly the problems of entry to marriage are most pressing. The sorts of things which we have in mind here are the problems of finding an appropriate partner, of knowing how to proceed in sexual relationships, and in general what may be termed learning the etiquette of sex. For example, young men

D

are expected not only to go out with attractive women, but in a number of social groups also to demonstrate their sexual prowess. The onus is on them to make the initial approach and to initiate sexual activity, although they may be uncertain as to how to proceed in such matters. Young women may also experience problems in this area, although of a somewhat different nature. They are not supposed to initiate sexual relationships as they are expected to be generally more passive in seeking a partner and in initiating sexual activity. They are normally expected to respond to the advances of the male and are faced in a slightly different way with the problems of 'how far to go' and 'what to do'.[1] It is not our intention to discuss these problems in any detail. Our purpose in introducing them into our discussion is to indicate that the adjustment to work is just one of a number of areas in which young people are likely to experience problems.

The entry into work crucially affects the changing relationships in the family in many ways. It serves as a visible indication to parents and children of the young person's new independent status. The wages from work free the young people from economic dependence on their parents and provide them with their own resources for their leisure activities thus giving them a greater control over such activities. In many cases the status of wage earner carries with it other implications for relationships within the family, for the wage earners' contributions to the family income give them rights and privileges not accorded to non-contributors, and a corresponding latitude of behaviour which they did not have before. Many young people remark on the way their entry into work affects their relationships in the family by giving them greater independence in relation to their parents, e.g. by allowing them to stay out later at night, and generally to make more of their own decisions.

GENERAL PROBLEMS OF ADJUSTING TO WORK

Against the background of these general considerations we can now consider the problems of adjustment to work while bearing in mind that the problems encountered at work often act as a catalyst and focus for other problems of growing up. One general set of problems will be those involved in 'learning the ropes'. These comprise two main types of problem. Firstly, those which are narrowly technical and consist of learning and mastering the work tasks. Secondly, the more general problems of learning the customs and practices which govern the relationships between people at work. These latter problems may initially be associated with psychological problems of adjustment, for example lack of confidence and uncertainty in relating to older workers, although these are usually soon overcome. While these general problems are present for all young workers, the forms which they take will differ from job to job and significantly between the three occupational channels which we have distinguished.

Another minor problem occurs when young people enter an occupation in which they cannot pursue some of the interests they had previously developed. In many cases young people develop particular interests during their school life, either through participation in school activities (such as metalwork or debating) or in the pursuit of hobbies at home. Young people with an extended career perspective are more likely to develop interests and skills of an abstract nature, for example an interest in arithmetical problems, while those with a short-term career perspective are more likely to develop interests of a more practical nature, e.g. carpentry. In contrast to these two groups, the interests which the careerless develop are unlikely to be rooted in their school activities and they are unlikely to expect to pursue them in their jobs. However, it is not always possible even for those young people with short- and long-term career perspectives to find work which will fulfil their interests. They may thus be forced to abandon such hopes if they are to make a career, and this may be unsettling for them, at least in the very early stages of their work experience.

Another general set of problems, this time of a serious nature, occurs when there is a disjunction between the young persons' expectations of work and the work in which they find themselves. That is, those situations where they fail to gain entry into the occupational channel at which they are aiming. There are many types of such disjunctions, the most obvious being situations in which home and school experiences vary greatly from those at work. This type of disjunction usually results from the young persons' failure to achieve the educational certification necessary to enter the jobs of their choice. Another is the situation referred to earlier where the disjunction first experienced between school and family continues into work. That is, those situations where families refuse to accept the definitions of the children's future work prospects conveyed at school and are unable to secure 'appropriate' work for their children when they leave school.

A final general set of problems are those resulting from *blocked mobility*. By blocked mobility we mean not simply those cases where the young workers fail to achieve a measure of career success, but also those cases where they discover that the occupation which they have entered does not provide the types of career opportunities which they were led to expect. This latter situation occurs more frequently than may be apparent at first sight, and it is particularly common among those who seek to make an extended career.

Although the general character of these problems remains the same, the ways in which they are experienced will vary from one type of young person to another. The kind of adjustments that the young people may have to make in the face of situations which do not support their self-image and orientation to work will be determined not just by the nature of the situation they face, but also by the type of self-image they have acquired. In short, the meanings of their adjustment problems will vary in accordance with the type of self-image and perspectives they have acquired and the type of work situation they are confronted with. It is to a more detailed examination of some of these circumstances that we now turn.

PROBLEMS ENCOUNTERED BY THOSE WITH A CAREERLESS PERSPECTIVE

The problems likely to be experienced by these young people entering careerless jobs are those associated with the day-to-day activities involved in their job and their level of pay. The main problems are not those of mastering new skills but rather those of learning to cope with their relationships with older workers, their subordinate position at work, and the boredom and monotony of the job. As their work offers neither promotion, security, nor the opportunity to acquire a skill, and indeed as they have never learnt to regard these as important, then whether the foreman is always 'breathing down their neck', whether they are on short time, and whether their job offers three or four simple operations rather than just one, all become important considerations in evaluating different jobs. Job changing provides one solution to these problems. Since the present is not experienced as a preparation for a long-term career future, the best solution may be to get another job where they may escape immediate problems or maximize rewards. In addition, it may be the only way in which they can experience any variety. Finally, as the major source of reward derived from such jobs is money, it makes sense to leave for a job that pays more.

The evidence indicates that these young people are likely to experience the 'problems' associated with their work more acutely after two or three years at work. On first starting work they often go through a 'honeymoon phase' in which work is experienced as providing freedom and independence, and most of them find work satisfying in the light of their recent experience of school. This is followed by a period of increasing disillusionment as the novelty of working full-time begins to wear off and the young workers have to learn to cope with the boredom and routine of their work. At the end of this discontented phase, as they enter their late teens and early twenties, most of these young workers are thinking seriously of 'settling down', of getting married and starting a family. It is in this period that they are more actively looking around in order to establish that they have the 'best' jobs possible—which for most of them means that they are earning as much as possible. Once this threshold is crossed and they enter 'full' adult status then they appear to become less discontented with their work.[2] This pattern of dissatisfaction is likely to be far more pronounced among the careerless than among young workers in the other two channels because their jobs tend to offer fewer areas of potential satisfaction either in terms of the interest they can hope to develop in their work or in terms of the rewards that they can expect from it.

There are two main ways in which these young people resolve their growing disenchantment with work as they come to realize that it will not provide them with the more general non-monetary satisfactions which they may have expected. The first of these is the adoption of what has come to be known as an instrumental orientation to work. That is, they come to look on work only as a means of making money, whereas when they first enter work they also view it as providing other satisfactions such as freedom from the discipline of school, working outside, and the like. These satisfactions increasingly become subordinated to monetary considerations and the young workers become willing to accept many unpleasant characteristics of work for the sake of obtaining high levels of income.

A second type of solution is to change jobs directly 'problems' are experienced. This should not be confused with changing jobs merely to maximize income, which is a product of an instrumental orientation. Rather, this type is more 'reactive' to immediate problems and often results in a very rapid sequence of job changes with eight to ten job changes in the first two years being not uncommon. It is these young workers whom the youth employment service and the employers are likely to define as having 'failed to settle' in work. We stress that this group or category is defined in this way *by the agencies* rather than by themselves. As we pointed out earlier, fairly frequent job changing is often a rational way for the careerless to solve their problems. Of course, some of this group may be experiencing severe problems, however we should not assume that frequent job changing is a reliable and accurate indicator on its own of such problems.

The frustrations of careerless work create more problems for the men than for the women, although they may generate similar levels of dissatisfaction and frustration. This is because the women can escape from work – even if only temporarily – as they start a family. As we have seen earlier, the wife-and-mother role tends to be seen by the women as their most important role. Closely associated with this identification are the attitudes the women hold to work and their expectations of it.

As they do not see themselves as the main breadwinner in their future family, their level of income is less important and they may be far more concerned with the kind and quality of the relationships they can establish with other workers.

More serious problems are experienced by those who fail to find a job. As we have seen, these young people are defined as 'failures' while they are at school, and they often look forward with anticipation to the freedom and independence that work will provide. When this is not forthcoming then it appears that their confidence in handling relations with others and their self-confidence take a further blow. From their point of view they have 'failed' again; this time to find the work that would enable them to maintain their longed-for independence. Even those who at school were also treated as having similarly limited abilities now appear to have some qualities that these unemployed young people do not have. Another and perhaps equally damaging blow to these young unemployed is that because they do not hold a job they do not have the same resources at their command as their contemporaries and hence their participation in leisure activities is restricted. This tends to undermine the only other area where they can establish support for the development of their identity. In this situation it is not at all surprising to see them failing to admit to the possession of any positive personality attributes or qualities. The consequence of long-term unemployment for these young people then is that their self-image as someone with ability, albeit somewhat limited, is undermined with the result that they have little self-confidence. This is compounded further by their continued dependence on their family and their inability to maintain 'normal' leisure activities.

While specific occupational tasks are not missed, continuous employment is an important factor in ensuring that they can obtain some meaning and satisfaction from their non-work activities. Some of these consequences may be mitigated in areas where there are relatively high levels of unemployed young people. In such areas group associations and activities may develop among the unemployed focusing around 'delinquent' activities which provide a source of mutual psychological support and meaning for them.

It should be made perfectly clear that it is common for some of these young people to experience short periods of unemployment as they move from one job to another, seeking to get the best they can for themselves in terms of the kinds of rewards and satisfactions that semi-skilled and unskilled work can offer. Such short spells of unemployment do not undermine their image of themselves as young people capable of finding and holding down a job; on the contrary they may even reinforce feelings of pride in the fact that they are not tied down but are free to move as they please between employers. However, the situation may be very different if the period of unemployment is prolonged, and it is young people from this channel who are most susceptible to prolonged unemployment during an economic recession.

Prolonged unemployment is likely to pose less of a problem for the young women. In the first place, as we have already indicated, work is not usually as important to them as it is for the young men. Secondly, the young women can contribute to the effective running of the household through taking over household tasks of various kinds which in some cases may even free their mothers to work. Further, such household work is seen as a normal part of their identity as women and can thus substitute effectively for work in a way in which it cannot for young men.[3]

The problems created by unemployment are complicated by a number of other factors for the children and grandchildren of immigrants. These are the same type of factors that we have discussed in connection with their school experience, namely: discrimination, poor command of English, and conflict between their home background and the world of work. The obvious effect of discrimination and a poor command of English is to prevent such young people from obtaining work or to make them more vulnerable to being laid off. We must, however, be careful not to overgeneralize. The term 'immigrant' covers a wide range of people with greatly differing cultural backgrounds and patterns of family life. Some children of immigrants from the West Indies, for example, may have aspirations that reflect the structure of opportunities in the West Indies and which may be incongruous with the opportunities facing them here.

Some in the face of discrimination or an initial failure to secure what they consider to be appropriate (skilled) work, tend to drop out of the labour market rather than seek careerless jobs which will pose serious threats to their identity. For some of them certain aspects of West Indian 'culture', namely that centred around the shebeen, may provide an alternative source of income and support.[4] Asian immigrants have to be differentiated into at least two types, those who are from a peasant background and those from a more affluent commercial and professional background. It is children from the former group who are most likely to enter careerless work.[5]

PROBLEMS ENCOUNTERED BY THOSE WITH A SHORT-TERM CAREER PERSPECTIVE

We will now look at the problems experienced by young people with a short-term career perspective. When these young people enter jobs offering such careers they are unlikely to experience the problems of boredom and frustration at work encountered by the careerless. The types of problems they face are more concerned with their immediate career future, and with ensuring that their employers provide them with the chance to learn the requisite skills that will provide for this. They know with a fairly high degree of certainty that if they can obtain such skills they will almost automatically reach the next step on their career ladder, which for many is as high as they wish to go. There may well be anxiety about securing the appropriate skills during the initial stages of their work, particularly if they find their time is mainly spent in 'mashing' tea or running errands, but this anxiety normally disappears as they begin to master their skills. In some cases, however, and particularly for those young people entering smaller firms, this initial anxiety may be compounded as they come to realize that they are not going to acquire such skills nor the job security and social status which accompany them. That is, they find themselves in a position of blocked mobility. This may be because the young people do not meet the standards the employer expects or because the employer has used the false promise of extended training to attract young workers to jobs they would not otherwise have entered. In such situations the young workers may find it difficult to come to terms with semi-skilled or unskilled work precisely because they have spent two or three years receiving initial support and elaboration for the way in which they see themselves and their work future. To find themselves suddenly confronted with a future in semi-skilled and unskilled work may prove to be particularly traumatic.

For those young people who find themselves trapped in such situations the eventual outcome is usually that they come to cope with their positions by modifying their self-images and orientations to work. This can be a very slow and painful process as it requires them to change what are often firmly entrenched beliefs about themselves and the way in which they relate to the world of work. From what little knowledge we have it appears that most of them attempt to maintain their self-image in a modified form by finding some way of putting distance between themselves and their work. Some of them do this by convincing themselves that they are only continuing in their job until 'something better' turns up. Others, especially those trapped in unskilled and semi-skilled work, are able to accept that they may stay in this type of work for the rest of their working days, but yet maintain their image of themselves as capable of 'better things' by seeing their present job as a deliberate choice on their part to maximize earnings. As we shall see in the following chapter the various 'helping agencies' appear to be generally unsuccessful in helping them make such adjustments, and so the success with which these young people cope is often largely dependent on the support they receive from their families.

Young women are more likely to be frustrated in their attempt to enter occupations offering a short-term career than are young men. Also, they are more likely to experience blocked mobility within such jobs. It seems, however, that they are able to accept and adjust to their work situation more easily, and hence experience less severe problems than the young men. This apparent ease of adjustment may be closely connected to the significance which these young women attach to work. Unlike the young men, they can opt out of the labour market for considerable periods in order to raise a family. As a result of this 'alternative', and the many constraints on these young women to accept it, it is less likely that they will have as firm a commitment to making a career as young men.

While situations of blocked mobility are most common in smaller firms, for those young workers entering the larger firms with well-organized training schemes, there may well be other problems. Because they have good facilities and are given individual instruction in the basics of their trade, they do not always have the initial anxieties about the quality of their training that the other young workers have. This does not mean, however, that their training is unproblematic, for they may well experience boredom and frustration as a result of the way in which the training is organized. More serious problems are likely to occur for them after they have been trained when the pride they have developed in their expertise may throw them into conflict with the production requirements of large factories which frustrate them in the 'proper' application of their skills. Two more problems experienced by these young workers concern their comparatively low rates of pay which may severely limit their leisure activities and create ambiguity over their status. Indeed this early phase can be very worrying until the situation with regard to their status and the type of training they can expect is clarified. Secondly, in those cases where night school is involved problems may arise from the resulting curtailment of leisure activities and the extra work. All problems of this sort focus around the difficulties of subordinating immediate rewards for those of the short-term future. In this respect they are clearly of a different nature to those every day problems experienced by the careerless.

For young people with a short-term career perspective the most common cause of severe (if not traumatic) problems of adjustment is where they have to enter unskilled or semi-skilled work. This may occur either because of their lack of qualifications, because of the level of competition in the local labour market, or because they become dissatisfied with their initial choice of work and leave it in an attempt to solve the more immediate problems it poses. Their entry into careerless work creates problems for them because they have been taught to see work as an area within which they can 'make something of themselves'. They now face a situation where the skills they have acquired are inappropriate and their potential is frustrated, and thus they see themselves as 'failures'. Work, which they expected to be a source of meaningful and satisfying activity, now becomes drained of meaning and represents a threat to the way in which they had learnt to see themselves. All this means that work which provides certain minimal levels of satisfaction for other young people is seen by them as demeaning, and threatens to undermine the image they hold of themselves. Some of the young workers caught in this situation try to solve their problems by persistently attempting to secure entry to an apprenticeship or similar type of job. However, this option is only open to them for the first few years of their working life due to age restrictions on entry to many occupations offering short-term careers. Moreover, the demand for these, especially the skilled trades, is far greater than the number of openings, and consequently a large number of such young workers are inevitably trapped in unskilled and semi-skilled occupations which create serious problems for them.

The problems created by entry into careerless work are likely to create tensions in their relationships within the family as well, although they are likely to be less severe for these young people than for those who are downwardly mobile from the middle class. They may encounter problems with their disappointed parents as a result of their perceived failure to find appropriate work. Also the conflict between perspectives encountered at work and in the home may create problems, particularly in so far as they lead the young person to question the values held by their parents. There are also likely to be disjunctions in the young persons' social life as they may find it difficult to maintain relationships with their school friends who have succeeded in entering careers. When these young people begin forming friendships with their careerless workmates and taking part in social activities with them, the anxieties this creates for their parents may lead to further tensions within the family.

PROBLEMS ENCOUNTERED BY THOSE WITH AN
EXTENDED CAREER PERSPECTIVE

For those entering the occupations that provide the chance for
making an extended career, the major problems they will face
at work will be associated with ensuring their continued success
within their career. The kinds of problems they encounter in the
course of their early work experience are thus somewhat similar
to those encountered by young people entering short-term
careers. That is, they are essentially problems about their
future at work. For them a great deal of the satisfaction they
derive from their work comes from the knowledge that they are
going to make something of themselves in the longer-term
future, and the hope that many have of becoming a member of
an occupational group of high status receiving relatively high
levels of monetary reward. The fact that such success is central
to the maintenance of their image of themselves as capable of
getting on in the world is likely to increase the anxiety which is
generated in the work situation. In some instances, e.g. in
highly bureaucratized organizations, the young people have in
front of them a fairly clearly defined career ladder in which
educational qualifications are frequently used as the criteria
for advancement up the ladder. In this situation the young
workers are likely to know where they stand in the race for
promotion and hence their anxiety will be focused on the
examinations and other formal criteria that influence their
rate of advancement.

In many cases, however, the career ladder is not clearly defined. Even where it is, educational qualifications may be used
in conjunction with other more nebulous criteria which even
those who have succeeded in reaching the top may find difficult
to define. Where there are no clear criteria for promotion, the
anxiety generated by the pressures to 'get on' at work are more
diffuse and often harder to handle because of their lack of focus.
In such situations the young people are constantly searching for
cues as to what is appropriate behaviour, what kind of qualifications they should be aiming for, and what it is that will
impress their superiors. In these situations the mastery of
interpersonal skills, such as projecting one's personality, come

to be seen as just as important as the mastery of technical skills.

A common problem facing these young workers is the experience of blocked mobility. The early phases of long-term careers are often characterized by work of routine and boring nature, as for example when office routines are being mastered. While the young workers may recognise the dull and boring nature of such work it is seen as nevertheless meaningful as a preparation for their future career advancement. If it is discovered that they will not be given such an opportunity, i.e. that they no longer have a chance of making something of themselves at work, what had previously been accepted as meaningful becomes just dull and routine. This typically occurs after they have been at work for a number of years and after they have invested considerable time and energy in mastering the initial stages of the career. Examples of such blocked mobility are 'trainee managers' who come to realize they are only travelling salesmen, or little more than office clerks. The transformation of self-image which such situations imply will be difficult to accept, especially because work is potentially more important for these young people than for any others. Once it is realized that the chance for advancement no longer exists work will lose much of its meaning, for not only will they be restricted to low status jobs, but they will remain in approximately the same position, with approximately the same levels of reward, for the rest of their working lives. That is, they can no longer be seen either by themselves or others as having the capabilities for making a career which they thought they possessed. Thus the experiences at work, after providing an initial elaboration and confirmation of their self-image and orientation to work, now symbolize 'failure' in the competitive struggle for advancement. Of course some young workers in this situation are able to overcome their problem by changing jobs, but this solution is often not feasible due to the age restrictions on entry into such occupations. Generally speaking, the longer the young workers stay in an occupation the more they become 'locked' into the job and the more difficult it is for them to move, so that what may appear an obvious solution is not necessarily available to all.

The point we wish to emphasize is that these 'failures' are often the inevitable result of the structuring of work and are not due simply to inadequacies on the part of young workers. It is often very hard for school-leavers to interpret accurately the career prospects realistically available to them, particularly as many employers tend to exaggerate the prospects they offer. This is particularly likely to occur in jobs which have no clearly defined set of specifications, although blocked mobility can occur even in jobs where the tasks are clearly defined, and where the bases for advancement are clearly specified. This is particularly the case for women.

There are two further situations which may create severe if not traumatic problems of adjustment to work for these young people. The first is where the young worker is obliged to enter semi-skilled or unskilled occupations.[6] This is epitomized by the grammar-school pupil who, because of his lack of educational qualifications and the shortage of openings for him, finds himself working as a labourer in a factory. From the point of view of such young people this creates a situation of considerable stress and tension. They now define themselves as failures, for they cannot make anything of themselves nor obtain entry into a career. The kind of training they received at school, and in particular the kind of 'abstract' skills they acquired, are inappropriate for the type of manual work with which they are now faced. The frustration they experience is compounded by the fact that they are doing the kind of work which prevents them from exercising those very skills in which they have learnt to take pride. Not only are their skills inappropriate, however, but so too are the values and standards by which they have learned to guide their behaviour. Although such situations create very severe problems, their occurrence is surprisingly low. It seems that middle-class parents are very capable of 'working the system' in such a way as to prevent their children from entering the more 'undesirable' careerless jobs.

A more common disjunction occurs when such young people are unable to find a job offering long-term career prospects and thus have to enter occupations that only provide the chances of making a short-term career. This normally happens for two main reasons: the young person may fail his school examinations, or the pressure of competition in the local labour market for 'middle-class' occupations may be so great that some of them will have to enter occupations on a lower rung of the status ladder. Either way they find themselves in an occupation that does not provide the career chances, the chance to better themselves, that they had always felt themselves capable of obtaining. In such cases they enter an occupation in which they cannot easily sustain the image of themselves and of the importance of work in their lives that they had previously acquired at home and school. In this second situation, however, the discrepancy between the image of themselves acquired earlier and that which can be supported by the realities of the work situation is not as great as in the previous case, for these young workers can still see themselves as capable of making some sort of career and of achieving a certain level of success at work. What is meant, however, by a 'career' and career 'success' in these occupations is so different from that which the young people had been led to expect that they may still find these occupations difficult to adjust to, creating tension and stress. Once again it should be pointed out that in such cases work which provides a relatively high level of satisfaction for the majority of the young workers who perform it may be experienced as demeaning by those who had always believed themselves destined for 'something better'.

Wherever there is this incongruity between the young person's experience of home and work then there is likely to be tension created in the relationships within the family or at work. This is clearly seen in the extreme case of the young man from the middle-class family, with a grammar school education, entering a careerless occupation. At work his relationships with his workmates will focus on the immediate situation, and the nature of his work experiences will make it impossible for him to differentiate his experience from theirs, in terms of future prospects. If he is to adjust successfully to the demands of the work situation and establish satisfactory relationships with his fellow workers, he must learn to attend only to the immediately given aspects of work and his relationships with others and not try to subordinate them to considerations for future career advancement. In this situation if the young person attempts to sustain the views and beliefs transmitted within the family, even though they are incongruous with the 'realities' of the work situation, then considerable tension is likely to be experienced in the relationships at work. If, on the other hand, he should attempt to develop a new perspective more in accordance with the situation he faces at work, and particularly if the parents refuse to accept such changes, then the relationships within the family will become more tense. In either case the young person is going to be faced with conflicting views of himself and the world which will inevitably create severe problems of adjustment.

The problems experienced by young women are somewhat more clear-cut than is the case for men. While there are a variety of occupations offering extended careers for men, for women State Registered nursing and teaching offer the majority of opportunities for extended careers. Of these teaching requires a long period of full-time further education beyond the school leaving age, and this is also the more normal mode of entry into State Registered nursing. Most other occupations which offer women the chance of long-term careers (e.g. the social services) also require full-time further education. Banking provides the best-known occupation which does not require full-time further education, although here the young women are likely to experience problems of blocked mobility. The effect of this narrower range of opportunities is that those young women who are unable to enter an occupation offering an extended career are likely to be made aware of their failure more quickly than their male counterparts and will thus spend less time attempting to achieve such a goal. This may allow them to come to terms with their situation more quickly, and to explain it in terms of the state of the labour market or male dominance rather than as a reflection of personal inadequacies. Even those women who succeed in entering an extended career are faced with problems not experienced by their male counterparts as they are likely to experience conflict between their wishes to pursue their career and to start a family.[7]

REGIONAL VARIATIONS

Before summing up the main points of this chapter we must
briefly refer to the effect of regional variations (discussed in
Chapter 2) on the nature of the problems experienced by the
young workers. Because of these regional variations the extent
to which young people experience the problems of adjustment
discussed in this chapter will vary from one part of the country
to another. Where there is a shortage of juvenile labour, as in
London and the South-East, the problems of unemployment
will be less severe and fewer young workers will be downwardly
mobile than is the case in those regions, such as the North-East,
which are characterized by a surplus of juvenile labour. Given
these regional variations and localized pockets of unemployment, fluctuations in the economy will have very different consequences for young people in different parts of the country.
A downturn in economic activity will bring a tightening of the
labour market in the South, which may mean that careerless
youths will find it more difficult to change jobs at the rate they
have done in the past. Those wanting to enter short-term or
extended careers will find greater difficulty in finding appropriate work, and they will also be more likely to experience
'discontinuities' on entering work. In some of the northern areas it
will inevitably mean that a higher proportion of those with a
careerless perspective will enter the ranks of the unemployed
directly they leave school. It will also mean an increase in the
proportion of young people moving out of these areas in order
to secure long-term careers. For those who remain it will lead to
a lowering of aspirations and an increasing number of disjunc-
tive experiences as many young people who are reluctant to
move have to accept a job in occupational channels below the
level to which they aspire.

One final point that needs to be made about the importance
of regional variations is that the existence of a relatively high
rate of unemployment in one locality over an extended period
of time is likely to bring about a corresponding adjustment in
the perspectives of young people. For those intent on entering
a career it is likely to lead to a lowering of aspirations, while
for those from a careerless background the consequences are

somewhat different. In the discussion so far we have assumed a realtively high level of employment and have assumed that it is realistic for young people to see as one of the advantages of careerless occupations the lack of commitments that they entail and the freedom to change jobs. In areas of high unemployment this will not be so, for a high rate of job changing is likely to expose the young person to the threat of prolonged unemployment. In this situation there is some evidence that what will be valued will be the chance to hold any job. Similarly, those who seek to make short-term careers are more likely to emphasize the security which having a trade gives them rather than the status or monetary rewards it may bring. A similar adaptation and 'narrowing' of focus will also occur for those entering long-term careers. Over the country as a whole, but especially in the North and to a lesser extent the Midlands, any downturn in economic activity is likely to bring about an initial increase in many of the problems that we have discussed in this chapter.

SUMMARY

We began by pointing out that the transition from school to work is one among a number of changes associated with the process of growing up. This general process is characterized by the increasing independence of young people, and, although it involves inevitable stresses and strains, does not normally create serious problems for them. The transition to work is clearly an important phase in this process, and in many ways acts as a focus and catalyst in it. On entering work the young people will inevitably experience certain difficulties in adjusting to their new situation. However, such difficulties, for example, 'learning the ropes' or getting on with older workers, are normally relatively minor and are quickly coped with. These difficulties confront young workers in all jobs although their nature and importance will vary from one channel to another.

There are two general situations which create severe problems of adjustment. The first of these occurs when there is a disjunction between the experiences and associated perspectives and self-conceptions of the young people and their experiences at work. The situations creating such disjunctions are those occurring when young people with a short-term career perspective enter careerless work, and when young people with a long-term career perspective enter short-term careers or careerless work. The common element in both these situations is that there is an incongruity between the perspectives held and the constraints or realities of the occupational position in which the young people find themselves.

The major source of severe problems for those in the careerless channel is prolonged unemployment. Although the job itself may not be highly valued by such young people, it is important for them to hold a job. This not only provides economic resources but also, as we have shown, has important social and psychological consequences for them.

It is important to note that in this chapter we have dealt primarily with those young people who are downwardly mobile, i.e. those who are moving into a stratum lower than that occupied by their parents. We have maintained this focus because these young people are the 'casualties' of the system of social selection that operates in this society and so are the ones that present themselves most frequently to the various helping agencies. They are the young people who in most cases would like to get out of their present situation. We are not implying that those who are moving up the social scale in relation to their parents do not also experience problems and conflicts. While their problems may be just as severe, they will want to learn how to cope with situations at work which their earlier experiences failed to prepare them for, and not to avoid them or escape from them. Such young people are the 'successes' of the system of selection, and the positions they move into at work may offer them greater rewards than either they or their parents initially expected and they may thus have every incentive to remain in their jobs. The subsequent anxieties and tensions involved in the process of learning to adjust to their new situation is more likely to bring them to the attention of their GPs than it is to bring them to the attention of the careers advisory service. Their problems, as they see it, are not with their jobs, which indicate their success in life, but with learning to cope with the new sets of relationships resulting from their jobs.

The second general situation which was identified as creating severe problems of adjustment is that of blocked mobility. This typically occurs after the young person has been at work for some time. The major problem created by blocked mobility is that after receiving initial validation and support for their expectations of work, the young people find that these will not be realized. This has two consequences; firstly, their work will lose a lot of the meaning it previously held for them. Secondly, it often raises serious doubts about the way they view themselves and may lead to feelings of self-doubt and inadequacy.

Our purpose in identifying the different situations which create serious problems of adjustment to work has been to indicate that such problems exist for young workers in each of the occupational channels we have distinguished. Severe problems of adjustment encountered by young workers embarking on short-term and long-term careers have often been insufficiently taken into account, due to the concentration of attention on the problems of the unemployed.

Notes

1 For a good general discussion of these problems see J. Gagnon and W. Simon, *Sexual Conduct: The Social Sources of Human Sexuality*, London: Hutchinson, 1974.

2 This increased satisfaction (or resignation) that is reported is reflected in the lower rate of job change of the adult workers in careerless jobs. See for example *Unqualified, Untrained and Unemployed*, Report of a Working Party set up by the National Youth Employment Council. Department of Employment, London: HMSO 1974.

3 It is also normally easier for women to gain part-time employment or intermittent temporary work than it is for men, and thus they are less vulnerable to genuine long-term unemployment.

4 The shebeens are illegal clubs focusing around illicit gambling, drinking, drugs and sexual activities.

5 A more detailed discussion of these points is to be found in S. G. Allen and C. Smith, 'Race and Ethnicity in Class Formation: A Comparison of Asian and West Indian Workers' in F. Parkin (ed.), *The Social Analysis of Class Structure*, London: Tavistock, 1974, pp. 39–53.

6 There is some evidence that where young people have established, either through their home or school experience, a strong sense of their own identity, they are able to reject semi-skilled and unskilled work as

unsuitable and use the Social Security income to maintain them while they engage on more creative tasks, for example leather and craft work. In this way their position as an unemployed young person does not threaten their sense of their own identity. This type of adaptation is most likely to be found among young people from a middle-class background.

7 The serious problems encountered by women who fail to enter long-term careers occur not with those who fail to proceed to the necessary full-time further education, but with those who succeed at this stage only to encounter failure on completion of such education. This is particularly severe for middle-class graduates from institutions of higher education for whom work has become a central area of achievement, but for whom there are relatively few opportunities. We thus get the situation where female university graduates can only find a job by obtaining secretarial qualifications.

7. Provisions made for Entry into Work

In this chapter we shall be concerned with the operation of the various organizations that young people come into contact with during their preparation for and entry into work. We are particularly concerned with the schools, the various government agencies, the employing organizations and the trade unions. Our intention is not to provide a comprehensive account of them but merely to identify the major constraints which affect the ways in which they operate with respect to young people. We shall then go on to consider the ways in which they relate to the three types of young person identified in Chapters 3, 4 and 5, and the problems discussed in the previous chapter.

The School

We shall begin by briefly reviewing the role of the school. We have already suggested that one of the important functions of the school is to channel young people into different sectors of the labour market. As we have seen, in the selection and preparation of young people for their future occupation the schools operate with a high measure of success. For the majority of their pupils, schools function to reinforce the self-image and orientation to work derived from their family experience which is later confirmed by their experience of work. For most of the remainder the school functions to modify their self-image and orientation to the world in such a way that it becomes congruent with the type of occupation for which they are destined as a result of their performance in the school. The end result is that by the time they enter work relatively few young people experience dramatic discontinuities or traumatic problems of adjustment.

Although the schools are successful in preparing the young people for work by transmitting the appropriate beliefs and attitudes, they are less successful in providing direct help and information about available work. This is hardly surprising given the limited resources available to the school and the many demands made upon the teachers, and in particular those generated by the pressures for 'success' in external examinations. Indeed, in most schools the provision of direct help in finding jobs is not seen as part of the school's responsibilities. Even in schools which do have careers teachers this function is seen as of secondary importance to the academic tasks. Most careers teaching is concentrated in the secondary modern schools and to a lesser extent in the comprehensives, and in only 15 per cent of all schools does careers teaching occupy as much as one-fifth of the work load of one teacher.[1]

Careers Service

The responsibility for providing help and information to young people in their last year at school formally rests with the Careers Officers employed by the local authority. This responsibility continues after the young people have left school. The position of Careers Officers is ambiguous and they operate within a number of constraints. The most important of these is that they do not have the authority within the schools to implement their objectives. They have an obligation to interview school-leavers and for this the schools, through the headmaster, must provide facilities, i.e. time for the interview, an interview room, and a report on the pupils. However, the success of the interviews depends to a large extent on the nature and quality of the information provided to them by the teachers, and any work they wish to do in the way of careers guidance depends on the co-operation of the teachers. It is the headmaster's decision as to how much, if any, of the time available can be 'spared' for careers work. Careers Officers are almost powerless in this relationship and have to rely on the headmaster for co-operation in implementing their objectives.

Given the constraints of the examination system this means
that in practice headmasters are prepared to devote time to
careers work only in so far as it does not compete with the
more academic subjects in the run up to the external examinations. Even when the co-operation of the school is granted, the
Careers Officers are likely to encounter further difficulties due
in part to their heavy case loads: with an average case load of
over 400 pupils there is little that can be achieved in terms of
personal vocational guidance. In addition, in the few schools
with careers teachers, there is often a conflicting definition of
responsibilities. Some careers teachers see their prolonged
contact with the child as providing the best basis for vocational
guidance. On the other hand some Careers Officers are likely
to claim this as their responsibility because of their special
expertise and knowledge of the local labour market, and see
the careers teachers' function to be the provision of information
about the students and the necessary administrative and support services.

Another source of ambiguity in the position of the Careers
Officers is the change in their function which has occurred in
response to changes in the labour market. The service was
originally initiated in the early years of this century (a period
of high unemployment) when the problem was to find jobs
and so place people in work. With the development of full
employment this function was expanded to include help for
young people in making an informed choice between a number
of available jobs. This, together with progressive dissatisfaction
with the system, led to a shift away from placement to a more
general concern with vocational guidance. This in turn led to
an emphasis on the educational and guidance aspects of their
work at the expense of their placement function. The shift from
the original concern to find jobs for young people to a primary
concern with careers guidance was symbolized by the adoption
(in 1973) of the title of Careers Officer to replace that of Youth
Employment Officer.

The idea of vocational guidance which informs much of the
work of the Careers Service is based on the belief that young
people should be able to develop their potential and find self-
fulfilment in their work through making a career. This, as we

have seen, is an inappropriate way of looking at semi-skilled and unskilled work, yet traditionally Careers Officers have catered mainly for young people entering such work. The shift towards vocational guidance has two important possible consequences for the way in which the Careers Officers relate to young people. First, it tends to direct them away from a concern with the careerless who form a substantial number of their clients, and whose work will not enable them to make a career. Thus they are directing their concern toward those with career aspirations. Second, it creates problems for the officers when dealing with those destined for careerless work, in so far as the vocational guidance concept hinders an understanding of the young persons' requirements of work.

The Careers Officers' relationships with the local employers, and their knowledge of the local labour market, act as another powerful set of constraints on the way in which they are able to perform their work. This raises the question of who, indeed, are the actual clients of the service. At first sight it seems obvious that the clients are the young people leaving school, and most Careers Officers adopt this approach. However, the employers are also in a very real sense clients of the service, and there is often a conflict of interest between these two groups. The young people may require particular types of jobs yet the Careers Officers' ability to place them in such jobs may be severely limited by the number of jobs available and by their relationship with the employers. If they are to provide guidance and help for school-leavers by placing them in jobs, the Careers Officers must have the co-operation of the employers. In order to maintain this co-operation they must be careful about the type of labour 'supplied'. Yet, as we have said earlier, there is no inevitable fit between the requirements of employers and the qualities and aspirations of those young people who are entering the labour market at any one time.

The Careers Officers' problems in matching the needs of employers and school-leavers are exacerbated by their incomplete knowledge of the labour market, for although they may believe that they have a perfect knowledge of the market, this is unlikely to be the case. While it is one of the Careers Officer's jobs to find out about the vacancies available in his or her area, it is difficult for them to remain fully informed of *all* the vacancies offered by *all* the employers at any given time. In particular they are less likely to be aware of all the vacancies available in the smaller enterprises. For reasons associated with the early development of the service, employers with semi-skilled and unskilled job openings, and in particular those which they have difficulty in filling, tend to use the service most continuously and intensively. Vacancies at the craft level and above are likely to be filled quickly, and for these vacancies employers frequently prefer that the young people take the initiative and apply themselves. This means that many of the vacancies that the Careers Officers have on their books at any one time are those provided by the 'worst' employers who have difficulty in retaining labour and who thus have a 'standing order' for labour.

Another complicating factor is that many more young people aspire towards jobs offering short-term careers than there are openings. This creates a dilemma for the Careers Officers. In their role as vocational guidance experts they may be sympathetic to such aspirations and feel that a young person without formal qualifications could be successful in, for example, an apprenticeship. In their placement role, however, they are subject to the constraints of the local labour market and their relationships with employers, and are forced to 'match up' the young persons' abilities and qualifications with the available openings. Because of this they may be obliged to direct the young person, through the provision of factual information about the labour market, to careerless work where vacancies are known to exist, and where the young person is more likely to be accepted by the employers. In this sense the Careers Officers perform the function of lowering some of the young people's aspirations. This will inevitably mean that many young people will find their advice difficult to accept and this may well account for the high proportion of them who have expressed dissatisfaction with the help and advice they receive.[2]

The problems discussed above are intensified by the fact that the Careers Officers are in competition with the local press, kinship networks, and more recently the Department of

Employment, as sources of information and placement. They are often used as a last resort by those young people who have failed to find a job through these other channels, and who thus may be difficult to place. Indeed it is in their interviews with the Careers Officer that many of the young people who are destined to be downwardly mobile and who will experience traumatic problems of adjustment are first likely to be made aware of their 'problem'. However, we must emphasize that it is very difficult for either the schools or Careers Officers to easily identify such people beforehand and so contribute towards alleviating the problems they will face. This is particularly the case when such difficulties are largely the result of problems at home. The teachers have no reason to enquire into relationships within the young person's family. If the teachers are not aware of problems in the family they cannot indicate them in their reports and so there is little chance that the Careers Officer will be aware of them when he or she advises the young person about which job to go for.

It is against this background of conflicting and often contradictory pressures that the function of the careers service must be seen. Firstly, it provides one of the most important sources of help, advice and information to young people about the world of work and especially the labour market. Yet, as we have shown, its effectiveness in performing this function is largely dependent on the help and the type of information received from teachers and employers. The evidence indicates that despite the difficulties under which the Careers Officers operate, about half the school-leavers find the service helpful. Secondly, the service performs the important function of job placement, particularly for those young people who have difficulty in finding jobs through other channels. About one third of school-leavers are placed in their first jobs by the service.

The Employing Organizations

The nature and type of provisions which the employing organizations make for young workers play a critical role in how the transition from school to work is experienced. The most important point to remember is that in our society the employers are not in existence to provide a service for the young workers, but to produce goods and services and, in the private sector, make a profit. The pressures they are under are those of the market. Their concern with the problems young people experience in making the transition from school to work is largely limited to the ways in which such problems of adjustment interfere with the efficient operation of their enterprise.

The extent to which they provide mechanisms for easing the transition varies greatly, and is directly related to their attitude towards the labour they are recruiting. In this respect a useful distinction has been made between the primary and secondary labour markets within which different firms operate. The primary labour market consists of those firms that treat their labour force as an economic investment. They are selective in their recruitment policies, in part because they do not want this investment to be wasted. They aim to attract the best labour available and to minimize rates of turnover, and as part of this policy they often establish close links with the schools and provide some form of induction for the school-leavers. Such induction courses may ease the transition by reducing initial apprehensions about work. Such apprehension may be further alleviated by the training programmes which these firms usually provide for all employees, even for those in unskilled work. Thus in these firms even semi-skilled and unskilled jobs may form part of a rudimentary career ladder in which some form of advancement is possible. The firms that comprise the secondary labour market primarily employ semi-skilled and unskilled labour and have a casual attitude to labour. They are most unlikely to provide induction schemes; they offer little in the way of formal training for those who join them; and make little provision for employee welfare. They are non-selective in their recruitment and are willing to accept high rates of labour turnover. Partly because they are less attractive to school-leavers they are the firms which are most likely to use the Careers Service in the continual recruiting of labour.

The net effect of these factors is that those entering careerless jobs, especially in the secondary labour market, are least provided for by their employers. Moreover it is in this sector of the labour market that most of the young people experiencing serious problems of adjustment to work are to be found. There are three main groups within this category. One group are those who, encountering problems in adjusting to a short-term career, attempt to resolve their problem by leaving their present job and entering this sector of the labour market. Another group are those who are identified at school as 'unstable' or having a poor school record and so are not considered by firms in the primary labour market. A third important group are the children of immigrants who, for reasons mentioned earlier, are also likely to find themselves in this sector of the labour market. All these are likely to be caught in a vicious circle. As they start to move from one firm to another, either leaving of their own initiative or receiving the sack, so they start to acquire what the employers in the primary labour market define as a poor or bad employment record and cease to be considered as possible applicants. In this way not only are these young workers progressively denied access to jobs offering extended or short-term careers, but their chances of entering those firms which offer security and training and a possible way out of the careerless labour market are progressively reduced.

Trade Unions

The trade unions, who might be expected to provide help to young people in making the transition from school to work, in fact do little for them. The main exception here is with some of the skilled unions, who traditionally have had an interest in controlling apprenticeships. An important factor for these unions is that these young people are seen to be making a lifetime commitment, and so they will provide a stable committed membership. For those entering unskilled and semi-skilled occupations there is little incentive for the unions to do very much because of the likely instability of their membership. Such young workers tend to enter the smaller firms and to change jobs more rapidly than older workers and so are likely to be moving through a series of jobs in which different unions recruit. Hence, even if they do join a union their membership in it is likely to lapse as they move into another job organized by a different union. Further, the smaller firms and those that comprise the secondary labour market are notoriously difficult to unionize, and in many cases there may be no unions organizing their particular workplace. In any case the unions see their responsibilities to their members as of a collective rather than an individual nature. Thus the action they do undertake is not geared to individual requirements but is of a broad and general nature, e.g. the attempts to extend compulsory 'day release' to all unskilled and semi-skilled young workers.

Other Organizations

There are a number of other organizations which may impinge upon young people at this stage of their lives. These include the Youth Services,[3] the Probation Service, the Employment Exchange, and the Social Security Service.

The Youth Services, which at first sight appear to offer an important source of support for young workers, in fact play a relatively minor part as they are primarily concerned with the provision of leisure activities. The only group of youth workers who play a significant part are the small number of detached workers. As with the Careers Officers they are in ambiguous positions and are subject to conflicting pressures. These produce a number of difficulties for them in the pursuit of their work, foremost of which are their limited access to resources; a lack of support and recognition by other agencies; and difficulty in establishing contact and support with the young people they are meant to help. Even when they gain the confidence of those young people experiencing serious problems upon entry into work, and understand the nature of their problems, they are relatively powerless to help.

Of the other organizations identified above, the Probation Service provides an important source of support and assistance for non-work problems for those young people in trouble with the legal authorities. As a result of the 1973 Employment and Training Act the Department of Employment has assumed some responsibility for the placement of young people. This will inevitably create further strain for the Careers Officers who now overlap with the Department of Employment in placing young workers, and this is likely to create further confusion for the young workers. The Social Security Service has the unrealized potential to provide an effective source of help due to the regularity of its contact with unemployed young people.[4] However, its function is defined in purely instrumental terms, and its members tend to see their role more as custodians of public funds than as agents for the people who use the service.

THE RELATIONSHIP BETWEEN ORGANIZATIONS AND YOUNG PEOPLE

Organizations and Extended Careers

In many respects the present system works best for the young people with an extended career perspective, for they are likely to share the same perspective as the representatives of the various agencies with which they come into contact. This does not mean, however, that there are no deficiencies in the way the present system works for these young people. One of the complaints that is most frequently voiced concerns what they regard as the neglect of their interests by their teachers, who are geared towards those who are staying on at school to prepare for entry into higher education. As the prestige of the school is measured in part by the proportion of its pupils that are successful in examinations, and in particular those leading to entry into institutions of higher education, there is a built-in pressure against the teachers taking much of an interest in those who are known to be leaving 'early'. Those young people who for one reason or another do not wish to pursue higher education and who seek direct entry into an extended career often feel that, compared to the effort devoted to ensuring the maximum entry into institutions of higher education, the effort devoted to ensuring that 'early leavers' make the correct choice of work comes a very poor second.

In other respects, however, these young people are fairly well provided for. The competition for their skills among the major employers is such that there is an abundant supply of information available about occupations that provide an extended career. Moreover, because they are entering a national as opposed to a local labour market, the entrance requirements to such occupations are fairly uniform for the different jobs throughout the country. Thus Careers Officers are more likely to have an accurate picture of the state of this labour market than they have of the market for other types of work. Also, as we have seen, their transition to work is smoothed by the initial period of training. For many, their participation in further education means that should they encounter problems they will have the resources of the institutions of further education available to them in addition to those which the firm may provide.

There are, however, a number of problems which are created by the way in which some employers attempt to attract such labour. Partly due to the competition for this type of labour, employers have a tendency to paint a rosy, idealistic picture of the jobs for which they are recruiting. While a firm may need five or six office workers with the prospect of one of them becoming a manager, it is always tempting to describe each of the vacancies as ensuring entry into management. The discovery by the unsuccessful workers after three or four years that this is not the case may, as we have seen, have traumatic consequences as they start to see themselves as having failed to make a career. Given the demand for this type of labour the practice of overselling job prospects is likely to continue. It should be pointed out, however, that even from the employer's point of view this had disadvantages. While it may initially attract the right type of recruits, as they become aware of their blocked mobility one of their most frequent responses will be to withdraw their commitment to their jobs and to lower their levels and standards of performance. From the young workers' point of view the consequences are much more serious. Because of the central importance which work holds for them, their failure in it is much more likely to contribute towards problems of identity than it is for young people in other types of occupations.[5]

Organizations and Short-term Careers

For those young people with a short-term career perspective there is little in their school experience that stands out as in need of radical change. They share in common with the other two groups a resentment of what they see as the childish manner in which they are treated at school, but apart from this aspect their school experiences are usually seen as useful by them. Because they accept some of the beliefs and values of their teachers with regard to work, their time at school is not necessarily seen as wasted. However, there is a tendency for the teachers to over-emphasize the importance of academic qualifications for these young people. While entry into work providing a short-term career is usually dependent on qualifications they are not always essential. As we have pointed out, the extent to which employers are likely to require paper qualifications is dependent on such factors as the size of the firm and regional variations in the state of the labour market. Also, there are usually a number of smaller firms who will accept young people for entry into a short-term career without formal qualifications. The emphasis which teachers place on qualifications may thus mean that some young people who fail to obtain their qualifications will move straight into semi-skilled work, unaware of the opportunities which exist for entry into work providing a short-term career.

A similar problem occurs in their relationship with the Careers Officers. As we have seen, these may be less aware than some of the young people of the smaller employers that offer short-term careers without insisting on formal qualifications. Like the teachers, they may believe that a young person with a poor academic record will be unable to obtain an apprenticeship (as indeed is the case with technician apprenticeship and entry into the larger firms) and consequently advise them to lower their aspirations. Generally speaking, however, these young people have much better facilities and a much greater range of information available to them than is available to those who enter careerless occupations. Firms tend to spend greater time and effort recruiting for these occupations, and provide more information either through leaflets or through individual speakers that the firms make available to the schools and Careers Service.

On entering work these young people, like those making an extended career, are likely to be involved in a period of training which will provide some continuity between their experience of work and school, and which will ease their movement into work. Should they encounter problems they also may have the facilities of the colleges available to them.

Organizations and the Careerless

The group of young people which receives least help from the schools when moving into work are those in the lower streams who are seeking to enter careerless occupations. We should emphasize that the school does not actively prepare them for their experiences of work as it does for the other two groups we have discussed. What 'preparation' there is stems from the unintended consequences of the way in which they are treated. Whereas the continuity experienced by the other two groups between school and work is of a positive kind, for these young people it is largely of a negative nature.

There are a number of reasons for the neglect of these young people. We have already pointed to the all-pervasive influence of the examination system and the ways in which this directs attention and resources away from this group of young people. Another factor is the clash of perspectives between these pupils and their teachers. The effect of these two influences is often to lead to mutual alienation between pupils and teachers. A final factor is the teachers' lack of information about careerless work and the openings available in it. In those schools which have a large group of pupils of this kind there have been a number of attempts to provide help and guidance for them, which have been allowed precisely because the influence of the examination system is weaker. For example, there have been attempts to introduce career guidance for these school-leavers, and to make their curriculum more interesting and relevant to them. However, by treating these young people differently there is a danger that they will be seen and see themselves as 'second-class citizens' and thus such schemes may prove to be counterproductive. Potentially of more use are the 'work experience' schemes whereby teachers and pupils obtain direct experience of industrial employment by working for a short period in factories and other industrial settings, which may provide them with a better appreciation of careerless work.

Despite these various efforts to improve the way in which the schools relate to these young people there are still serious deficiencies. What these young people need is practical help in improving their knowledge of the local labour market; in learning how to cope with official forms; in improving their knowledge of their rights and obligations in relation to their future employers; and in knowing how the local employment exchange and social security systems operate. They need to learn the social skills involved in handling interviews; they need instruction on which of the jobs open to the unskilled are likely to provide the chance for advancement; on what trade unions are and how they function; and on what the variations in wage rates are. This type of practical information is essential to them if they are to make what from their point of view is the best of their work experience. In a sense this information is all the more important because these young people are not catered for by the firms, largely because of the ease with which they can be recruited. Thus the firms do not provide as much information about the nature of these jobs as they do for others. In addition the local press do not run special features on the more mundane 'dead-end jobs' when they produce their careers features on the opportunities offered by local firms to school-leavers. When the school fails to provide young people in other channels with information about available employment, they can make use of these alternative sources of information. For these young people, however, there are no such alternative sources apart from the personal experience of relatives and friends.

We suggest one reason why teachers do not provide this type of help is that their experience of work cannot provide a basis for advising these young people. We should stress that the deficiencies do not stem simply from a lack of knowledge on the part of the teachers. What is needed is not simply more information about careerless work on the part of the teachers but also an appreciation that the values which have guided them in their own careers are inappropriate for young people who wish to enter semi-skilled and unskilled work, and, to a lesser extent, those entering short-term careers. Thus, for example, to tell young people entering unskilled work that they must work hard, stick to their jobs and behave themselves, because this will enable them to 'get on', is completely inappropriate. It is, however, sound advice to someone entering an extended career.

The main reason for this failure lies in the differing life experiences of the careerless and their teachers. The ideas of the world of work held by the teachers is characteristic of that found in extended careers. For them the central aspects of work are seen to lie in the ability to fulfil oneself, and the chance to demonstrate personal worth and prowess by moving up the career ladder. The need to demonstrate competence at work together with the value of loyalty to the organization create pressures which serve to tie them to their jobs for fairly lengthy periods of time. Indeed, job stability may be a requirement for promotion. In these circumstances it is not surprising that it comes to be seen as a virtue that may be rewarded by career advancement. Such a view is reinforced for them in their everyday behaviour, and by their friends and colleagues who share similar views. When confronted by young people aiming at entry into careerless occupations there is a danger that they will generalize from their experiences of work and apply their personal values in evaluating them. Thus they may view the young people's emphasis on the immediate rewards to be derived from work and their disregard of possible long-term rewards as a sign of immaturity, rather than of a deep-seated perspective.

There are two mutually reinforcing sources of this insensitivity to the careerless young people's views and requirements. By the criteria used for evaluating long-term careers, all careerless work is seen as the same in one crucial respect – its failure to provide the means of realizing one's potential or of making a career. These negative characteristics may be so great in the eyes of the middle-class viewer that the many significant differences between such jobs are largely overlooked. While, for example, it is seen as legitimate for a young person seeking entry to an extended career to limit his choice of jobs to those which meet his requirement of 'meeting people', a similar restriction of job choice by a young person looking for careerless work is often denied legitimacy because such jobs are *really* 'all the same'. The paradox is that those requirements which are seen as legitimate for discriminating between jobs which provide a career are not seen as legitimate in the context of careerless work; even though these are the only means of discriminating between them!

This failure to apply the same criteria to both groups is closely related to the ways in which teachers and other professionals view the personal characteristics of these young people. These are the young people who are manifestly the 'failures' of the system, and they are viewed as such. Further, their failure is seen largely as the result of inadequacies on the part of the young people themselves rather than as a product of the educational and occupational systems. These are the 'thick', 'lazy', and 'indifferent' who are seen as incapable of 'fulfilling' themselves through work partly because of these personal inadequacies and partly because of the nature of the work itself. This is, however, a misconception. It may be just as important from their point of view for these young people to be able to maximize their interpersonal skills through finding a job which allows them to meet people (e.g. a bus conductor or shop assistant) as it is for someone seeking work providing a career. We see no inherent reason or justification to generalize from the lack of 'technical' qualifications to a concomitant lack of capacity for 'fulfilment of potential' through work.

In many ways the considerations we have dealt with above also hold for the Careers Officers, for their personal experiences and their concern with careers guidance push them away from a concern with the careerless in a number of ways. Further, as we have seen, the Careers Officers are constrained not only by the 'capabilities' of the young people but also by the job openings in the local labour market, of which they are unlikely to have a perfect knowledge. Thus the wishes, likes and dislikes of this type of young person are less likely to be respected by the Careers Officers when they are endeavouring to place them in jobs. In part this is due to the fact that the Careers Officers may know less about some jobs available than the young people themselves. Faced with only a limited number of openings the Careers Officers may frequently have to direct young people into jobs they do not want. In part this is also due to the inability of the Careers Officers to appreciate what the young people see as important differences between such jobs. What all this means is that the young people build up a series of beliefs about the character of the service which may adversely affect their use of it. For example, one theme that frequently crops up in investigations is the view that the careers service is primarily a means of recruiting cheap labour for employers and that it is not particularly concerned with the interests of the young people. If Careers Officers are to gain their respect and co-operation they must have a realistic appreciation of the young people's distinctive view of the world. Unless they acquire this their effectiveness will be greatly hindered, for the young people become critical and distrustful of the agencies when they offer what is seen as unrealistic advice based on a lack of understanding of their problems and a refusal to listen to them.

It is not an easy task we are setting. The professionals' involvement in extended careers means that their perspectives are inevitably orientated towards career requirements, and so it will be difficult for them to use a drastically different set of assumptions when dealing with the problems of the careerless. We are not suggesting that all professionals working with careerless young people are unaware of and insensitive to their views and requirements. However, even the sensitive professionals are subject to constraints which make it very difficult for them to help these young people effectively. To alter the ways in which professionals view the young people, although bringing about some improvements, is not sufficient in itself to bring about major changes. To make any major improvements and alleviate many of the problems that are to be found in this area will require action on a broader basis, aimed at changing the relationships between home, school and work depicted in the second chapter. We consider this in the final chapter.

Because of the ease with which employers can recruit and

train young people for careerless work they pay little attention to such young people and invest little in them by way of training. The lack of induction schemes and lengthy periods of training means that for these young people the transition from school to work is more abrupt than for the other two groups we have discussed. It also means that they do not have access to the various sources of help and support which are available to the other groups. Also, the work experiences of these young people are qualitatively different, and in particular authority relationships are of a different character. The supervision of these young people is directed at the ability to perform their work and they have little chance to bring the difficulties they experience to the attention of those who control them at work. This creates problems not only for them but also for management, as it may lead to a high rate of turnover as the young workers attempt to solve their problems through leaving. We suggest that if the young people are given a chance to express their views, and if provision is made for handling their problems, this will to some extent lead to the eradication of some of the problems of both management and workers.

ORGANIZATIONS AND DISCONTINUITY

Let us now look at those who experience serious problems as a result of discontinuity or threatened discontinuity in their movement from school to work. There are two main groups to consider here, those whose aim to enter work offering a career is threatened, and those aiming at careerless jobs who cannot find work.

The first group is frequently not identified while still at school. Their problems usually stem from examination failure at the end of their school careers which prevents them from entering the occupational channel for which they have prepared themselves. One option available to them is to make use of the colleges of further education. This option, however, is not open to those from families with more limited resources, and hence is most likely to be taken up by those young people whose parents are following an extended career. For those aiming at entry into occupations providing an extended career the colleges of further education provide a chance of obtaining the academic qualifications which they failed to obtain at school. For those aiming at a short-term career there are more alternatives open to the girls in further education than there are for the boys. These range from 'O' level courses and nursery-nurse courses to typing and secretarial courses. By using the colleges of further education young people may be able to postpone or avoid the problems which entry into a lower occupational channel would create. Where they are successful in taking this second chance provided by the colleges all may be well. If, however, they fail again, then they have merely postponed the full impact of the 'problem' for one or two years, and for these young people who encounter serious problems of adjustment to work at the age of 18 or 19 the present system provides little support. Moreover, we suggest that at this age the problems may be more difficult to cope with because of the extra time and effort which have been invested in further education to no avail.

For those young people who do not make use of the colleges the present system provides little help for dealing with their problems. As we have seen, to adjust to work in a lower channel than that for which one has been prepared requires a substantial change in the person's self-image and orientation to the world. Inevitably this involves changes in family and other non-work relationships which together may take considerable time and emotional effort, and which require the kind of intensive support which can only be obtained from a fairly close and continuous relationship. Given their heavy case load, it is unlikely that the Careers Officers will be able to establish such relationships with many of their clients. Where such relationships are most likely to be established is with those young people who are downwardly mobile from the middle class, due to the similarities in their perspectives to those of the Careers Officers.

For those young workers with a careerless perspective, serious problems are encountered when they leave school and become unemployed. The Careers Service has few resources with which to combat the problems caused by prolonged unemployment. There has been some success with group work in attempting to restore or develop the self-confidence and self-respect among the young unemployed. However, the Careers Service does not have the manpower to undertake group work on a large scale, and in any case this is only of limited value if the young people remain in a state of unemployment. While the Community Industry Scheme may have helped some unemployed young people, given the magnitude of the problem (particularly in areas of high unemployment), the limited resources available, and the tendency of some other professional workers to view such young people as 'hopeless cases', there is little that is done for them.

Failure to secure appropriate employment may or may not be associated with serious problems of a more general nature. In coping with these more general problems the Careers Officers and the other agents we have discussed are very limited in terms of what they can do. In the first place it may be difficult for them to determine the depth of the problem as experienced by the young people. As we stressed earlier, the transition from school to work often acts as a catalyst for other problems often, but not always, associated with family relationships. Young people may not wish to divulge these to someone whom they see as responsible for advising them on work. Similarly, even if they suspect that the young person's problems at work are part of a broader set of tensions and conflicts, these professionals may not feel competent to deal with them. In any case, they are frequently not in a position to offer the kind of support necessary to enable the young people to come to terms with their problems.

A Note on Special Cases

While it is hard to be precise, we think that there is a 'hard core' of young people who experience and create problems at school and at work perhaps because of psychiatric problems. These are the young people who are seen by the agencies as having special employment problems: they are variously referred to as 'semi-literate', the 'socially disadvantaged', or those 'at odds' with the system. What distinguishes this group from other careerless young workers is their rapid rate of job changing and what appears to be an inability to form stable relationships at work. These are the young people who frequently, but by no means always, come from families in which relationships between the members are characterized by acute conflicts and tensions. Because the numbers involved are small in absolute terms (one estimate puts them at about 40,000 for the country as a whole[6]), and because the agencies have only recently become aware of them, there has been little systematic evidence to draw on in discussing these young people. From the reports of the agencies that are concerned with them, the typical career pattern of this type of young person emerges as follows. The child is brought up in a family that is either a working-class 'problem' family or a middle-class family in which relationships are subject to acute tensions. These feed into and contribute towards the child's failure at school. The child's attitude towards the school may be manifest either as an attitude of resigned apathy, or as one of overt conflict and frequent truancy. At the end of its school life the young person moves rapidly through a series of jobs, either being sacked by the employer or 'leaving for no adequate reason', with periods of employment interspaced with periods of unemployment. In times and areas of high unemployment these young people will not be recognizable by the agencies as having special problems as they will become an indistinguishable part of the unemployed.

While we do not wish to deny that these young people have serious problems, what we wish to stress is that their problems are frequently those of establishing any lasting relationships with others. It must be realized that chronic job changing may be symptomatic of a more general problem, and that these young people do not necessarily see work as creating special problems. At the moment the agencies are not equipped to help them with such general problems. The social services and social workers are not geared towards the needs of single young workers, and the various government agencies, such as Social Security, cannot help them. Their situation contrasts dramatically with that of the young people who are successfully making their way towards an extended career and are receiving further and higher education. For these young people in the colleges and universities there are the welfare officers, student counsellors and student health services to support them should they encounter psychiatric problems. By contrast, for these young careerless workers there is nothing. Even the recently introduced Community Industry Scheme (1971), which has provided help, support and training for some unemployed young people, will have had little impact on the young people we are discussing here. Their problems are not those which can be resolved by acquiring habits of industrial discipline or elementary occupational skills.

While this group is largely drawn from a careerless background, we suspect that it also includes a significant proportion of those who are downwardly mobile from the other groups. The ranks of these young people are thus swollen by some of the others we have discussed, who may join them for an indeterminate period of time. The important point to be made is that the boundary between them and other young workers is permeable. Given support and opportunity some of these chronic job changers may obtain satisfactory work and move out of this category, while some of the young people who start their working life by spending a fairly long period with their first employer may move into the ranks of the chronic job changers later on, perhaps as a result of sexual and emotional problems they encounter in their non-work lives.

SUMMARY

In the first section of this chapter we looked at the specific part played in the transition from school to work by a number of organizations. We suggest that although the schools are successful in preparing young people for work at the attitudinal level, they are less successful in providing direct help and information. The reason for this was seen to lie in the limited resources available to the school and the competition of what are interpreted as more relevant academic criteria. The main responsibility for providing help and information for the young people lies with the Careers Officers. However, due to the many constraints under which they operate and the ambiguity of their position these professionals are only partially successful in meeting the considerable demands placed on them. Neither the employers nor the trade unions provide much in the way of support for young people making the transition from school to work. All of these organizations make greatest provision for those entering careers and there is little or no provision made for those entering careerless occupations.

In the second section we considered in a little more detail the relationship between these organizations and those young people experiencing continuity in their transition from school to work. Once again we found that those young people making careers were much better provided for than those who were not. In this context we suggested that the provision of an initial period of training played an important part in smoothing the transition from school to work. The neglect of the careerless young people is seen to result not only from organizational factors but also from the failure of those in positions of power and responsibility to appreciate their views and needs.

In the final section we considered those who experienced serious problems in the transition from school to work and concluded that there is little which is effectively done to help them cope with their problems. The main exception is that the colleges of further education may provide a second chance to those who are prevented from entering the careers of their choice due to examination failure.

Notes

1 *Careers Education in Secondary Schools*, Education Survey 18, Department of Education and Science, HMSO 1973, p. 16.

2 We do not mean to imply that Careers Officers deliberately set out to 'lower aspirations'. Rather, our point is that in the performance of their job they will inevitably do so for a proportion of their clients whose aspirations, for whatever reasons, are unrealistic. It is hard to be precise about the responses of young people to the Careers Service as reports vary. A national enquiry of school-leavers found that just over 50 per cent of their respondents found their interview with the Careers Officer very helpful, and just under 40 per cent found it not helpful. Schools Council Enquiry *Young School Leavers*: HMSO, 1968; Table 11.7.3., p. 131.

3 The term Youth Service is used here in a broad sense to cover the various services that are available to young people either through central and local government provision or through the efforts of voluntary organizations.

4 The main exception to this are the unemployed children of West Indian parents.

5 While this often creates serious problems for them, there is very little that the helping agencies can do for such young people. Until recently the Careers Service has had an upper age limit of 18 placed on those it could help, which further reduced the sources of help formally available to these young people. As the cause of blocked mobility is the organization of work, the only way in which it can be solved, if at all, is through a major transformation of the way in which work careers are organized.

6 *At Odds*, Report of the Working Party of the National Youth Employment Council, HMSO, 1970.

8. Social Policy and Social Change

LOCATING THE PROBLEM

In this book we have attempted to show the mutually reinforcing effects of experiences in the home, at school, and at work on the development and transmission of the different ways in which young people come to view themselves and their world. We identified three main types of perspective. The first of these is to be found among families occupying the least advantaged positions in our society, and is characterized by its focus on the *immediate present*. The second is to be found in those families in which the husband pursues a short-term career, and is characterized by its focus upon the *short-term future*. The third is to be found in those families in which the husband is making an extended career, and is characterized by its focus on *long-term planning and deferred gratification in the pursuit of long-term future rewards*. The problems experienced by young people holding these different perspectives vary, but for all of them their entry into work is likely to serve as a catalyst and focus for the more general problems of 'growing up' while at the same time posing new problems. For most young people their entry into work does not cause them severe problems. Such problems are, however, likely to arise in those cases where there is a clash between the perspectives transmitted at work and those held by the young person. This is most likely to occur when the young people are downwardly mobile relative to their parents.

The various organizations involved in the young people's transition from school to work are most successful in providing help and information to those young people who are planning to enter work which offers them the prospect of making a career. They are least successful in helping the careerless and those who are downwardly mobile (frequently into careerless occupations). Our analysis indicates that it is precisely these groups who require the most help. It is difficult to determine the size of the problem due to the lack of systematic research. However, we can say that approximately one half of those young people who enter careerless occupations originally aim at jobs other than those which they finally enter. While not all of these will be downwardly mobile a significant proportion of them will consist of those young people who are hoping to enter jobs offering the prospect of a career.[1] Even among those young people who look forward to their entry into careerless work a significant proportion will experience deprivations resulting from the character of their work. This is indicated by the rapid increase in the number of these young people who come to see the income provided by careerless work as the only significant reward offered by their work, despite the fact that many of them initially seek non-monetary rewards.

It is for these reasons that we focus on changes which could be made in the position of the careerless in our society. We argue that what is required if their position is to be improved is a change in the broader relationships between work, home and school depicted in this book. Our concentration on the careerless does not mean that the provisions made for young people in other categories is adequate. However, it is the careerless youths who have least provision made to help them. Further, their work problems are part of more general problems they face as a result of their position in our society.

In terms of the dominant beliefs of our society, their jobs are the least desirable, which means that the young people who enter careerless occupations are looked down upon and judged as failures. While they may cope with these beliefs by rejecting them, nevertheless they will be aware that many people will judge them as failures and look down on them because of their jobs. Another set of problems they face stem from the fact that many of the jobs they do are 'objectively' undesirable. The conditions of work are often poor and dirty, and the jobs provide little or no chance to develop skills or to take an interest or pride in work. During a downturn in economic activity the young people who enter these jobs are especially vulnerable to unemployment. In times of full employment these are the jobs that are immediately vacated and into which immigrant labour has in the past been recruited. What all this suggests is that while these young people may be conditioned to these jobs through their experience of school and express satisfaction with them, they do so because they have no alternative.

A further problem that confronts these young people and their families is the limited material resources available to them because of their jobs. These place a number of restrictions on family and community life (explored in Chapter 3) which affect the kinds of relationships that can be developed in these contexts. In turn family life is an important factor leading to the children being placed in the lower streams of the schools. At school and work yet further problems confront these young people, problems of identity that stem from failure of school and work to provide a sense of achievement for these young people. These problems are more acute for those who experience long periods of unemployment. We suggest that their involvement in delinquent activities, e.g. soccer violence, and the activities of the skin-heads (and before them the 'Teddy Boys') is in part a by-product of their experience in these areas. Although the links are not fully understood it is fairly clear that one of the functions of these group activities is to provide a sense of identity and achievement which cannot be gained through their work or school activities.

These then are some of the more general problems that face young people in the lower channel. What our analysis indicates is that the attitudes and outlook they develop in response to them will be transmitted to the next generation, which is likely to experience the same deprivations and arrive at similar solutions. Because of the mutually reinforcing nature of the experiences in the different areas of their lives it will not be possible to provide an immediate solution to the problems of the careerless. What is needed is a co-ordinated attack on the problems facing them rather than the present piecemeal approach. Although there have been a number of attempts to introduce changes in other areas (which we discuss in the next section) we suggest that the area in which the maximal impact can be made is that of work, since changes here will have pro-

found and all-pervasive effects on the ways in which young
people experience their world and will powerfully influence
family relationships.

AREAS OF CHANGE

I : *Education, Family and Leisure*

The most concerted effort to intervene in the mutually reinforcing effects of work, home and school has been directed at
the educational system in an attempt to provide 'better' or more
equal educational opportunities for young people from this
type of background. These have failed to make a significant
change precisely because the occupational structure is organized
in such a way that almost 30 per cent of each generation have
no option but to enter careerless occupations. As we have
already seen, there are more young people seeking to enter
occupations that provide a career than there are positions
available and this is one source of problems for young people.
Thus, the attempt to provide the careerless with the opportunity to obtain the educational qualifications necessary for
entry into a career does little to improve the situation and indeed
may exacerbate it unless accompanied by concomitant changes
in the occupational structure. What may have happened is
that attempts to provide more equal educational opportunities
have intensified the competition for jobs that provide a career,
and in so doing created increased rates of *both* upward and downward mobility since the proportion of such jobs available to
young people has only increased very slowly. The recent change
in emphasis in educational philosophy is likely to create more
problems of this kind, for if successfully implemented it will
increasingly unfit young people for careerless work by encouraging them to take a more active part in questioning their
environment and in the determination of their lives. These are
not characteristics which employers of this type of labour look
for in their employees, nor are they characteristics which are
particularly congruent with careerless work. What is clear is
that changes in the educational system by themselves cannot
bring about any radical change in the nature of these jobs and

the rewards which they provide. To be effective, such changes must be geared to changes in the work situation rather than merely hoping that changes in the school will somehow bring about a change in the nature of work.

Partly as a response to the perceived failure of changes in the educational system to bring about a more egalitarian state of affairs, attention has recently been focused on the family as the source of inequality and deprivation. In particular 'deficiencies' in the ways in which children are brought up in careerless families are seen as the main cause of inequalities, and attempts have been made to 'compensate' for such deficiencies. In practice this has involved the special provision of nursery education for the children of such families in the attempt to 'enrich' their early experiences. We feel that such attempts can be only partially successful while the occupational structure maintains its present shape and the character of careerless work remains unchanged. Moreover, given the low level of income, poor housing, and general insecurity which confront the careerless families, it is unrealistic to expect that the parents will have the time and energy to treat their children in the same way as they are treated at the nursery school. Thus while the introduction of nursery school education for careerless children has beneficial effects for both the children and their parents, it may create problems in parent-child relationships due to the conflicting perspectives transmitted in the nursery school and the home. It seems to us that the changes in educational philosophy at the secondary level, to the extent that they have been successful, have also contributed to the generation of interpersonal problems within careerless families as the young people come to challenge the ways in which they are treated and in which their families are organized.

A less clearly articulated attempt to improve the situation of careerless youth and to solve the problems they create for others has been via the provision of leisure facilities. However, the knowledge we have of these youths indicates that it will be insufficient merely to provide more and more of the same type of facility that is already provided for other groups. We already know that these young people will not use them, or the youth services generally, if it means that they will have to subordinate themselves to traditional forms of authority. What is required is experimentation and inquiry into the kind of provision that will be effective, and in particular the kind of provision in which the young people themselves can play a responsible and meaningful role.

Although we have been critical of these various attempts to change the position of careerless youth, we do not mean to imply that they are irrelevant. What we wish to stress is that they can only be successful in the context of more radical changes in the work situation of the careerless.

II : Occupation

In this section we will focus on changes which can be made in the organization of careerless work in general, and will not directly consider the situation of careerless youth. We have already considered specific problems created for young people by careerless work in the preceding chapters and indicated that they are largely caused by the insecurity of such work and by the lack of autonomy and involvement it allows them. To alleviate the problems which careerless work creates for young people it will be necessary to do more than introduce such minor changes as induction schemes. What is required is a fundamental change in the character and organization of work.

The kind of changes we have in mind are those that would transform the character and rewards of what is now semi-skilled and unskilled work. There are a number of ways in which this could be done. As far as the market situation of these workers is concerned, changes aimed at decreasing job insecurity and providing prospects of a stable income with the possibility of some real increase are required. Since career structures are primarily organizational forms there is no reason why they could not be introduced into such jobs to provide incremental increases in pay based on length of service. Another possible strategy is to break down the traditional distinctions between unskilled, semi-skilled and skilled work by providing the opportunity for movement from less skilled and interesting work to more complex and highly skilled work.

Such movement could occur as the workers acquire the appropriate competences during the course of the work, and would inevitably involve a certain amount of training. What we are suggesting here is that selection into skilled work should not be restricted to the early years of the working life, but that entry into skilled work should remain an option in later life.[2] In addition to the creation of such 'career structures' changes are also needed in everyday work experiences, in the enlargement of jobs, in the introduction of greater control by the worker over how the jobs are performed and in the decisions that are taken about them. Changes such as these would generate greater commitment to and involvement in work, and are required if any substantial change is to be brought about in the day-to-day experience of unskilled workers. For example, the provision of a stable and secure income that has the prospect of a progressive increase in the future is likely to change the attitude of careerless workers by releasing them from the immediate day-to-day problems they currently experience, thus enabling them to plan for the future. Similarly, we suggest that if they are called upon to play an active part in decision-making at work then their attitude towards authority and their exercise of it in their own family will gradually change.

The changes we have suggested have been introduced to a greater or lesser extent, and with varying degrees of success, in a number of countries. The best example of the provision of career structures for semi-skilled and unskilled workers is to be found in Japan. These were introduced largely to combat the difficulty which the larger employers faced in attracting and retaining a permanent committed labour force in the years following the Second World War. Regardless of their skill level all permanent employees are offered security of employment and the possibility of progressive increases in salary contingent upon satisfactory work performance. The increases of salary are not only geared to task performance, but also reflect length of service.[3]

There have been a variety of ways in which 'job enlargement' has been introduced into the organization of industrial work.[4] The most simple strategy has been to increase the number of tasks carried out by each worker. While this may increase the variety of tasks performed and create more interest in work it does not necessarily have these consequences, and in any case is limited in its effects. A more far-reaching strategy has been pursued in Sweden where Volvo have introduced what is referred to as a 'team system'. This involves a degree of control by the workers over the way in which they divide the work among themselves and the methods they use in performing their work and monitoring its quality. We should emphasize that the employees are not directly involved in major decision-making and that the main focus of the experiment is to increase the attractiveness and interest of the work. The effect of these changes on the workers is still to be evaluated. As with the Japanese innovations, the Swedish experiments are a product of economic and social pressures. More specifically they are a response to high levels of absenteeism and labour turnover, vulnerability to market and technological changes, and trade union pressure to obtain improved working conditions and more interesting work for their members.[5]

The introduction of workers' participation in decision-making processes has taken a great variety of forms ranging from attempts to give workers greater control over their work tasks to their direct involvement in policy decision-making. Most European countries are experimenting with some form of workers' participation, although with varying degrees of success and commitment. In the Federal Republic of Germany (West Germany) workers have legally been involved in the decision-making process since the Second World War as a result of government legislation providing for works councils and worker directors. Such participation is largely restricted to personnel and social matters. In most industries 'works councils' are elected by the workers although in the heavy industries the situation is different, for here the trade unions act as the workers' representatives. However, in both situations the workers themselves seem to have very little chance of directly participating in decision-making processes.[6] The most extensive involvement of workers in the decision-making process is in Yugoslavia where it proceeds through the election of workers' representatives to policy-making committees which can exert considerable influence on all phases of decision-making. These include not only personnel and social matters but also investment decisions, distribution of income within the enterprise, and technical decisions. Reports indicate that a significant proportion of workers actively participate in the scheme.[7]

By comparison with the experiments carried out elsewhere, in Britain employers, trade unions and government have done relatively little. Nevertheless the organization of unskilled and semi-skilled work has been affected in a number of ways by government action. The Industrial Training Act (1964) has encouraged firms to introduce training for many of the semi-skilled workers who previously received little or no training. Other legislation, by introducing compulsory redundancy payments, has put pressure on employers to think twice before casually sacking employees, whilst more recent legislation has given employees the right of appeal against wrongful dismissal. The 1975 Industry Act may bring about changes in authority relations in industry that will affect the unskilled workers. The Department of Employment, through its Work Research Unit, is encouraging industry to experiment with changes in the organization of careerless work. These are only small steps, and they are likely to remain so as long as the issue of the character of unskilled jobs and their consequences for those who perform them are not raised to the level of public debate and overall government policy.

If any change is to be made in the work position of the career-less in our society it will require the active participation of the trade unions in bringing them about. Yet trade unions have tended to avoid raising questions about the content and organization of unskilled work as an issue subject to collective bargaining. There is no inherent reason why the concern with career structures and their shape should be a monopoly of the unions catering for skilled work or the middle classes, or why only such workers should have job security. What such action requires is a fundamental change in the attitudes of the unions and a restructuring of the trade union organization which at present tends to reflect traditional divisions in the occupational structure established in the first half of the nineteenth century.

While the unions have played a relatively minor role in affecting changes in the traditional organization of industrial work there are groups of workers who have taken the initiative in effecting such changes, as a result of economic necessity. For example, the takeover of shipbuilding on the Clyde and the number of 'workers' co-operatives'.

What we are suggesting in this section is that fairly radical changes be made in the organization of the division of labour and authority relations, and that these changes be directed at eradicating many of the least desirable aspects of semi-skilled and unskilled work. Our brief overview of developments in other countries indicates what can be done to bring about significant changes in market situation and experience of work. We cannot explore all the implications of these schemes for the British situation, but a number of general points emerge clearly. First, direct control over the job tasks and organization can make work more interesting and rewarding and lead to significant changes in self-esteem and the ways in which workers view their competence.[8] Secondly, the Yugoslav experience, although it still has problems, shows that changes in traditional authority relationships between management and workers can be brought about and shows that workers can effectively participate in policy making. Perhaps the major failure of the Yugoslav experience is the low level of participation of unskilled workers. This seems to be a result of the failure of worker participation to transform the organization of work and the division of labour within the enterprises. Thus the character of careerless work has remained largely unaltered under most of these schemes. However, as the Volvo experiment shows, it is possible to change the character of such work and to actively involve 'careerless' workers in making decisions about the organization of their work. Once this has been achieved they may play a more active part in other areas of decision-making.

The reason we have paid so much attention to possible changes in the organization of work is our conviction that work is central in maintaining the disadvantaged position of the careerless in our society. As our analysis has shown, the low level and uncertain nature of the income which careerless work provides places severe constraints on family life and serves to concentrate attention on immediate concerns and problems. This concern is reinforced by the work experiences of the career-less, which also affect the way in which their children are brought up. In turn this affects the children's performance at school, leading eventually to their entry into careerless work. In this way the perspective which careerless work plays such a large part in producing and maintaining is transmitted from one generation to the next. Despite the importance of these changes in the work and market situation of the careerless, they would not be sufficient in themselves to bring about the desired improvements, and to be effective require supportive changes in the areas of education and leisure.

SOCIAL POLICY AND SOCIAL CHANGE

There are a number of factors which are likely to hinder any attempt to bring about the kinds of change we have advocated in the previous section. The most important of these is the lack of any clearly formulated policy to deal with the problems of the careerless. We suggest that a major reason for this is the failure to appreciate fully the close association between career-less work and other social problems. As far as the problems of careerless youth are concerned this lack of an overall policy is exemplified by the great variety of agencies involved in dealing with various aspects of their problems. In addition to the agencies discussed in the preceding chapter there are a number of government departments which are concerned with the 'problems of youth'. The Home Office through the Police and Probation Services is concerned with the delinquent and crimi-nal activities of these young people. The Department of the Environment, through the Ministry of Sport, is interested in soccer violence. The Department of Education and Science is formally responsible for the provision of educational facilities for these young people, although the effective decisions with regard to matters such as truancy and violence in the school are delegated to the local authority and the schools themselves. It is also concerned with the provision of leisure facilities through the Youth Service. The Department of Health and Social Security is involved with these young people through the provision of social services, although again this is organized at the local level. The Department of Employment is concerned in a number of ways with the employment and training of these young people. This brief listing clearly indicates the large number of agencies that are in one way or another involved with young people. What it does not indicate are the continual changes in the functions and responsibilities of the various departments and the lack of co-ordination between them. This fragmentation of effort and responsibility results in the problems of careerless youth being treated primarily in terms of the problems created by them for others, and only secondarily in terms of the problems experienced by these young people themselves.

Another important factor which would hinder change is that the type of changes we are advocating will entail the diversion of resources from the more advantaged sections of society, and this will inevitably create opposition. The skilled unions are likely to oppose the attempt to upgrade unskilled work because it will be seen as negatively affecting the position of their members. The employers of unskilled labour in the secondary labour market will inevitably oppose changes that affect the low cost of their present labour policies. The Conservative Party may well be fearful of the consequences of providing greater economic security for the unskilled, in that this may be seen as reducing their 'incentive' to work. Given this range of potential opposition it is naive to suppose that the changes we advocate could be brought about quickly.

The success with which social change such as we advocate here is brought about seems to depend both on public awareness of, and sympathy towards the problem, together with sustained political pressure. An instructive illustration of the importance of these factors is the comparison between the attempts of two significant groups within the careerless category (women and immigrants) to alter their position in society. The problems caused by and for the children of immigrants are relatively recent in origin and are mainly the result of the influx of Commonwealth citizens from the West Indies, India, Pakistan and East Africa into Britain. Such immigrants largely find themselves confined to careerless occupations and to the poorer residential neighbourhoods of some of the industrial cities. Partly because of their minority status, and partly due to their initial unfamiliarity with the workings of British society, little attention was paid to the problems of these groups although the problems they were seen to cause for others received some publicity. These groups exerted little sustained political pressure on government agencies partly because of their relatively powerless position and partly because of internal divisions within the category of immigrant. Finally, while it is known that such people were discriminated against in many areas of life, including the occupational sphere, such discrimination is very hard to prove conclusively. The lack of 'teeth' in the Race Relations Act (1968) reflects these factors, as does its implementation. Thus the Act does not appear to have been very effective in preventing discrimination and thereby creating more opportunities for immigrants to enter occupations offering the prospects of a career, or in securing greater security of employment for them.

The situation of women contrasts in many ways with that of immigrants. Although most women who work are in careerless occupations where they form the majority of careerless workers, women are by no means a minority group. Also, a sizable proportion of women are engaged in work which provides for a career. Such women have provided the leadership for the long period of agitation and political pressure on the government to change the disadvantaged position of women in our society. Further, it has been easier for them to prove their case since discrimination against them in terms of differential rates of pay, restriction on entry to various occupations and blocked mobility has been clear and not denied. Thus the women had only to prove that the reasons for such discrimination were unfounded whereas the immigrants have first to prove that discrimination exists, and then that it is illegitimate. The greater strength of the Equal Pay Act (1974) and the Sex Discrimination Act (1975) indicates that the position of women is more powerful than that of immigrants. It is of course too early to know how far these will affect the work opportunities open to women, or how they will lead to changes in the work situation other than the provision of equal pay.

Despite the differences between the two groups their experiences show that a sustained and concerted effort is required to bring about changes in the position of groups in society, and that such changes occur only slowly, and over a long period of time. The apparently greater success of women in changing their position seems to be due to the greater effectiveness in organizing and in mobilizing a large proportion of the society in support of their cause. We argue that if the situation of the careerless in general, and of careerless youth in particular, is to be altered what is required is a sustained and concerted effort to raise their problems to the level of public awareness together with an explicit and integrated policy for dealing with their problems. The question to be answered is where the pressure for such a policy will come from. We suggest that the two most obvious areas are the Youth Service, especially that section concerned with careerless youth,[9] and those trade unions which cater primarily for careerless workers.

SUMMARY

In this chapter we have focused on the ways in which the position of the careerless could be improved. In doing this we have concentrated primarily on changes that could be made in the organization and character of careerless work because we feel that work plays a central and all-pervasive part in the generation and maintenance of the problems experienced by the careerless. By adopting this focus we have inevitably ignored problems experienced by other types of young worker. In particular we have ignored the problems of blocked mobility and downward mobility. However, the suggestions for improvement in the work situation that we have made would clearly go a long way towards cushioning the effects of downward mobility into careerless occupations by young people initially aspiring to make a career. They will, however, do little to alleviate the problems associated with attempts to cope with the sense of personal failure created by such downward mobility. As long as social prestige is linked to work such problems will invariably be created. As far as we can see the only way to cope with these problems is some system of indivi-

Social Policy and Social Change

dual counselling, which is almost completely lacking at the present time.

We have suggested a number of strategies aimed at bringing about change in the character and rewards of careerless occupations. In particular we focused upon the introduction of career structures, job enlargement, and worker participation in policy-making. Given the close interrelation between work, home, school and leisure that we have pointed to, changes in the work situation must be supported by changes in these latter three areas. One of the reasons we have concentrated on the changes in the work situation is because we feel that there has been an over-emphasis on these latter areas as the place where change should be made. This over-emphasis is in part a result of the relative ease with which changes can be made in the provision of educational and leisure facilities as opposed to changes in the work situation.

While we anticipate resistance to implementing fundamental changes in the work situation, we maintain that such changes are essential if any meaningful improvement is to be made in the position of the careerless. We would not however expect immediate and dramatic results from them. One reason for this is that such changes will have only limited effects on adult workers whose perspectives are already well established. Their major impact would be on succeeding generations as they influence family relationships, the transmission of perspectives, and future work prospects. Further, one would not expect changes in the nature of family relationships to occur overnight as a result of changes at work. While work experiences play a central role in the determination of the outlook of family members and of authority relations within the family, other influences also play a part. In particular, family and friendship networks and community relationships have an important influence. As the core of the problem is the transmission of relative deprivation and its attendant consequences from one generation to the next, it will take a long time before changes have a significant effect. It is precisely for this reason that experimentation and action should take place immediately. In a book of this sort we cannot go into the detail necessary to spell out all the implications of what we are saying as they work themselves out in practical policy. Indeed at this stage this is not what is required. The immediate problem is to raise to the level of public discussion the relationship between semi-skilled and unskilled work and the problems it creates for the careerless and for others. Only once this has been done can we start to focus on the changes that can bring about and alleviate these problems.

Notes

1 Maizells reports that in the Willesden enquiry only 55 per cent of those in semi-skilled and unskilled manual occupations originally wanted the job they eventually entered. This compares with a figure of 86 per cent for those in apprenticeships. In the Leicester enquiry 49 per cent of the young workers who entered semi-skilled and unskilled work gave reasons for entering their first job that indicated they were positively attracted to it. The corresponding figure for those who entered apprenticeships was 72 per cent.

2 This strategy is equally applicable to the 'higher' levels of the occupational structure. For example, there seems to be no inherent reason why highly skilled hospital nurses should be prevented from acquiring some of the skills possessed by non-specialist physicians through on-the-job training. Similarly there is no inherent reason why Health Visitors should not acquire the skills of the social worker.

3 R. P. Dore, *British Factory, Japanese Factory: The origins of national diversity in industrial relations*. London: Allen and Unwin, 1973.

4 For a detailed examination of the various problems raised by the strategy of 'job enlargement' and employee participation in decision-making, see A. Fox, *Man Mismanagement*. London: Hutchinson and Co., 1974, pp. 94–121.

5 Because the Volvo experiments are so recent there has been no academic evaluation of them. We have been forced, therefore, to rely on material produced by the firm itself. See, for example, P. G. Gyllenhammar (President of Volvo), 'The Team System at Volvo', *Social Science Research Council Newsletter*, 27, April 1975.

6 'Federal Republic of Germany', Workers' Participation in Management Country Studies Series, *International Institute for Labour Studies Bulletin*, 6, June 1969, pp. 94–148.

7 P. Blumberg, *Industrial Democracy: The Sociology of Participation*. London: Constable, 1968, pp. 168–234.

8 Blumberg, op. cit., after an extensive review of 'workers' participation' concludes that 'There is hardly a study in the entire literature which fails to demonstrate that satisfaction in work is enhanced or that other

generally acknowledged beneficial consequences accrue from a genuine increase in workers' decision-making power' (p. 123).

9 There have been signs that the government is becoming aware of the need for some co-ordination of efforts in this field and is attempting to develop a general policy towards youth. See, for example, 'Provision for Youth', Department of Education and Science Discussion Paper, February 1975.

Appendix:
Selected Case Studies

The following recent case studies drawn from our files cannot be representative of all young workers, but they have been selected because they illustrate particularly well some of the main points we have made with regard to each of the perspectives. They were also selected partly because these young people could articulate their experiences clearly. To ensure confidentiality all names have been changed.

THE SHORT-TERM CAREER PERSPECTIVE

John

John is 17 and the elder of two children; he comes from a 'respectable working-class background'. His grandfather was a factory hand. His father started work as a warehouseman and worked his way up to become the manager of a small factory. As a result of the father's success the family had recently moved into the more affluent suburbs of the city although his mother continues to do 'outwork'. At the time of the interview John had been at work for a year and was still living at home. He was educated at a secondary-modern school where he did not experience any major problems and clearly saw himself as fairly bright and capable of getting on.

He describes his experience as follows:

It was streamed. When I started I was in the second stream and I came in the top four of the class and went up to the first stream in the second year. After that I was in the first stream all along. I came second one year out of the whole class and thinking then I knew it all then, I went and fluffed all the exams for the next two years and came nearly last in the class. I thought, well I've got to buck my ideas up and so I did and worked what I call reasonably hard and managed to retain a position about mid-way through the class. As for exams, I wanted to pass them. I wanted to stay on and take 'A' levels although my parents tried to convince me that it wouldn't suit me and so I suppose in the end because I didn't do too well in exams I turned to their way of thinking. In the last six months I flogged my guts out to get my exams. I only passed two out of the six but I got Grade 4 or the equivalent through the CSEs.

Although he did reasonably well at school and realized the 'value' of education he found himself in conflict with the school authorities. The way in which he reacted to his problems with the authorities was clearly very different from the responses of the lower streams whom he did not see as having the same abilities as himself.

In the fourth year they started to clamp down on discipline and they were making it hard for the pupils, y'know trying to enforce school uniform and we were caned for petty things like walking across the car park because it was out of bounds – I got that – I got caned for walking across the car park. That was the bit that got me at first. . . . We rebelled the only way we could which was politically which I thought was the best way at the time, political rebellion. . . .

In the lower streams they didn't want to know – In a way I suppose they didn't really understand to the extent that we did – I'm not saying they were thicker than us but they just didn't realize the difference at the time between the different political parties and different political views.

He complained that while he was at school he was given little help and guidance about entry into work although this was primarily because he intended to stay on. The information which was provided he found of little use:

There was a programme on the tele called *Know What to Do* or something on a Tuesday and they (school) took us to see that but I thought it was pretty pathetic. They gave you all the good aspects of the job and never showed you the bad aspects and you find that a lot of the kids couldn't figure it out what was wrong about it. I think they tended to plug the Army, Navy and Air Force a bit too much.

The teachers asked us if we were going to stay on and if we were then they didn't bother with giving advice about work. I thought I was going to stay on and then decided when I got the results that I was going to go out to work. So I just went out and got the first job I could.

He found the Careers Officer of no help:

Believe it or not I went into his office and he says I'll write off to one or two firms for you and he said he'd get me in touch with (a Technician's) course in engineering and I waited until the end of July for a letter from him, but never got one – Then I got this job I've got now and they had the cheek to send me a letter just after Christmas to say that if you are not enjoying your job come and see the Careers Officer he will put you right and I felt like writing a letter back and saying up yours.

In thinking about possible employment he only considered jobs which offered him a skill and the possibility of a future career:

I didn't want to be a mechanical engineer because I couldn't stand metalwork. I thought about car mechanic but I didn't think it would suit me. I wanted to be a civil airline pilot but my eyesight wouldn't let me. At one point I was crazy about joining the RAF but then I went all pacifist objection and changed my mind. I didn't want to go down the mines – the money's good but that's about all.

In the absence of help from formal agencies he found his job through the local paper and accepted it because it was

the first job that came along. I was interested in aircraft and I was looking through the paper one night and they asked if you wanted to be an aerospace engineer, if you do contact X, which is the firm I work for. So I wrote off and they wrote back and gave me an interview.

While it was obvious that the initial reason for entering the engineering trade was his interest in aircraft, it was clear that he had other considerations 'at the back of his mind', and that these served to 'lock' him into his job:

At one point three months ago I thought of jacking this job in and going packing in the shoe factory – wouldn't consider that type of work now. Well with my job I feel as though I've got some sort of secure future – the fact it's going to teach me a trade and when I've learnt the trade I can leave the firm if I don't like it and get a very good job in another firm and the point is that if you've got your exams, if you've had an apprenticeship you've got shop-floor training. If you ever want to go into office work or become an executive the opening's there if you've got your exams.

163

He describes his work experiences to date, and the minor problems associated with them as follows:

I worked for a week at the factory to get used to the way the factory runs and learn about what the factory does. I'm in the first year of training. There's three parts. In the first it's just basic engineering – filing bits of metal. Then it's up to machining – welding – lathing, turning and milling and they do teach you at the Tech. to do things like grinding machine tools. I've been there eight months – it's like a big school workshop. On the third part you go on to specialized jobs that is more like factory working and that's what I'm looking forward to.

I found it so much like school that it got on my nerves the first six months. They treated you like kids – as if you knew nothing. It's only that you're younger than them and they are supposed to know better – and even if you do know something they don't want to listen. The discipline was a bit like school, they enforced a few pathetic rules occasionally. I look upon myself as being mature enough to act like an adult, although at this engineering training group there are some who go around vandalizing the place.

It tends to get slightly boring – you stand by one machine all day machining one particular job to get it perfect and if anything goes wrong they just look at you, throw it in the bin, and say 'do it again' and that's when it starts getting boring when you attempt it two or three times. It tends to upset a lot of the lads.

For the first five or six months I was really bored – they threatened to sack me – I thought well, what am I going to do if they sack me, if it goes round to my next job that I've been sacked for lack of effort then I'm in a bit of a mess, so I bucked my ideas up. After Christmas I had two large pay rises. I thought well I'm in a better position now. I started to enjoy the job instead of hating every minute of it.

There were obviously tensions in his relationship with his parents which were present during his schooldays, and these were aggravated by his entry into work and the problems he experienced there. He felt that his decision to leave school had been

one nil to them sort of thing – it was the first goal to them. Mum and Dad thought it (the job) would be good for me, they asked me if I enjoyed it and I said yes. I lied – because I didn't want to upset them and then after a while they could see it was getting me down. I was getting more and more depressed. I couldn't care a damn about anything. I just wanted to be on my own or with a friend – they didn't like that. In a way I did my utmost when I was out at work to get back at them. I've grown my hair long – I went round in jeans and dirty clothes and things like this. That upset them and made them ashamed of me and I felt in a way that I was getting my own back. I found myself in a bit of a state and then I suddenly popped out of it. I suppose as I matured a bit more I could see their point of view.

His thoughts on the future are a mixture of fantasy and reality.

I'm going to see how many exams I can pass and I'd like to get up to HND and do a year's practical work and then I want to resign and travel. That is unless I get married. If I get married it's a bit different, I could do five years and become a fully-qualified man.

Janet

Janet (21) comes from a 'respectable' working-class family consisting of her parents, herself and her younger brother. They live in a predominantly working-class area on the outskirts of an industrial city. She was allocated to the lower streams of a secondary modern school which created a number of problems for her, none of which proved insurmountable largely due to the support of her parents who were convinced that she should enter office work. She describes the central features of her school experience as follows.

There were four streams A, B, C, D. I stayed in C all the way through. They didn't teach you much. I was pleased to get out, it wasn't the sort of school that takes very much interest in you.

Her main problems with school were in the last few years, largely due to her refusal to accept the definition of her capabilities:

I put in to stay on for GCE and they turned me down and then after about three months they came back and said would you like to come and take them because we have a place for you and I just said no. Having been refused the first time I was just not going to bother.

Both her teachers and Careers Officer assumed she was in-capable of office work:

when she (her English teacher) knew I wanted to go into an office she said I would never make a typist – that put the mockers on it – I was a bit upset.

We had a careers advisor and all she talked about to the girls was factories and shops and wasn't interested in anything else, and I wanted to go into an office because I'd seen the sort of factory life with me mum and it didn't appeal to me at all. It was a complete waste of time because she didn't tell me anything. She said she would try and get me an interview for a job – we waited for about four months and then we saw an advert in the paper for Grimshaws (a family firm) for juniors to train as typists. I went after that and got it off my own bat. The Personnel Officer gave us a test and I got the job. My parents went with me, they were pleased about the job.

Janet's account of her work experience highlights many of the characteristic features of short-term careers. Her job pro-vided a fairly lengthy period of training leading to the acquisi-tion of transferable skills and also proved to be of some intrinsic interest.

I went into the job as a junior, they sent me into day release at the college. I took my English exam at college and passed it. I took 3–4 typing exams and passed them, and I ended up in a typing pool and got to be a senior audio-typist which at the time was interesting because I didn't know what other jobs were going. I stayed there for four years, two years of which were the training period as a typist. I got on well with everybody, there was nothing I disliked. It did get boring, the pay was low but you stay because everyone was so friendly and they taught you and you feel as if you owe them an obligation to stay as long as you can.

The main reason she left this job was in order to fit in with her boy friend's schedule. He was working forty miles away. She became a 'temp', but quickly became disillusioned.

You don't get the big money they say you are going to get. It's very disappointing. They send you all over the place and don't give you expenses and in some places you are looked on as an underdog – make the tea and do this and do that. You've not got the status. Then I saw this advert for the Health Centre and applied.

Her work at the Health Centre renewed her interest in the
work although it made her more aware of the limitations her
lack of qualifications imposed upon her work prospects. However, she felt it was too late to try to acquire further qualifications as this would disrupt her relationship with her boy friend.
She has thus decided to subordinate her future work prospects
to those of her intended husband.

Since I've worked with the Health Visitors they've got to trust me
and if they are out and they have a client coming in I can go out
and reassure them that a Health Visitor will come and see them.
That's more interesting than anything, I'd love to get in with the
people and talk to them but I just don't know how I could do that
because I haven't got the qualifications. I've thought about going into
nursing but that would restrict my social life. With my boy friend's
job it's not the sort of job I could take up now. If I'd done it when
we first started going out that's fair enough because I would be a
qualified nurse by now and perhaps do a Health Visitor's course
but now it's a bit late to go.

Janet's entry into work did not create any problems for her
relationships within the family. Indeed, it was mainly due to
her parents' support and encouragement that she was able to
combat the school's negative definition of her as only suited for
careerless work. As in the case of many other young women the
focus of strain in her family relations seems most likely to arise
around her marriage plans rather than her work career.

As for her plans for the future, these centre primarily on
marriage and her future husband's career, although Janet does
not intend to stop work indefinitely.

I'd like to stay in a job as long as possible and get as much out of it
as I possibly can – until I'm about 25–27. Hope to be married, have
a house and a family – but I don't want to have a family until I've
got a house and everything that I want – I will stop work until the
kiddies are old enough to go to nursery. I expect to go back to work.
I don't intend to stay at home, I'd get bored, waiting for my husband
to come home from work, doing his dinner and ironing his shirts –
it's OK for so many years but the novelty just wears off, I don't
think I could stand it.

THE EXTENDED CAREER PERSPECTIVE

Trevor

Trevor (19) has been upwardly mobile in relation to his father, who was a sergeant in the Armed Forces. As a result of his success in the 11-plus examination his parents, and in particular his mother who had received a private education, developed high aspirations for him. After moving through different grammar schools he was found a place in a direct grant school when his parents settled in a country town. His account of his experiences at this school indicates some of the problems of coping with the tensions associated with upward mobility and the difficulty such young people have in making 'correct' decisions at school. He says:

During the time I was at Marston's it all changed and became private which is very handy to be able to tell people but I don't really feel that I merited it because y'know the Forces paid for most of it. It was streamed – three sets and I was streamed into the lowest. I always remember in the first term I was told that I was on a term's trial and if I didn't do well I would go to the secondary modern up the road, and I worked bloody hard and came sixth for that term and of course I stayed on. After that I started to let things slip, but not too drastic. I worked enough to get by and stayed where I was. Once in the third year there were five sets – I was in sets 5 and 4 for all my subjects until 'O' levels – I didn't work much at all, there were too many things going on – too many distractions at the school. There was a lot to get involved in and I regret now that I didn't get more involved as I could have got a lot more out of it. I made a bad decision in the fourth year ... I chose sciences because I was very interested in skin diving because my father does it and I thought ideal – skin diving and marine biology and I'll be a marine biologist. I'm a bit naive. I don't blame the school (but) I didn't have much advice from the school. It was entirely left up to us what we did so I chose science – looking back it was not very far-sighted because I just can't handle maths. Then I went into the sixth year and then I realized I had made a mistake in choosing sciences. I started to do the 'A' levels, Sociology, Business Studies and Biology because biology was always the subject I had been good at for some reason, and I realized that it only went as far as 'O' level and that I would never make an 'A' level biologist.

I re-took maths twice and failed both times. Did first year 'A' level, I didn't really work and I was advised at the end of the year to get out and find a career now and not waste another year and get bad 'A' level grades which I feel was partly good advice and was partly part of the headmaster's notion to get rid of all day boys which is what he is doing now. I feel angry that I was convinced to leave rather than to work harder, admittedly I had wasted a year but I could have made up for it.

The sudden termination of his school career due to his academic failure presented Trevor with the problem of securing appropriate work, i.e. work which would provide him with an extended career. As we shall see later it also created problems with his parents. After a temporary summer job his first serious job was in September:

I realized it was time I started putting money into the house if I was going to continue living there. I virtually took the first thing I could find. A friend of mine who was an accountant said that a company whose accounts he did were looking for someone to do their purchase ledger accounts. So I took this job and it was an office job. It was deathly boring. I was completely green. I hadn't the faintest idea what was going on. I began to twig that there was a system that the accounts were drawn up at the end of every month. It was two months before I realized what I was doing and this was near Christmas. I hadn't really settled into the job and it was obvious that I wasn't going to and apart from that it was just something I was not suited to. So I started to look for something else.

At this point he saw a Careers Officer.

He said well with your sort of qualifications and your sort of attitudes you would probably be advised to go into something like hotel management or retail management, something in that line. I opted for retail management and joined White's (a national retail organization) at Christmas 1972.

It is significant that during his interview Trevor never mentioned the possibility of entering skilled manual work although it appeared that his parents at one time had planned for this. It is clear that Trevor's school experience was crucial both in Trevor's failure to consider skilled manual work and in changing his parents' ideas about his work future. When he was asked about entering an apprenticeship by the interviewer he replied:

It was not something which was ever mentioned at the school because basically the school was my life for five years. My parents were quite happy for me to be there. Quite pleased. If I had got my 'A' levels and been accepted for university they would have been delighted, so they never considered an apprenticeship for me. Although I do remember a life insurance policy they had on me matured and they said that at the time they took it out they thought it would just be sufficient to buy a basic set of tools for me for my apprenticeship.

Trevor was able to describe the career ladder at White's in great detail. One started as a stockroom trainee and moved through a series of stages each implying a different status in the organization, but not carrying greater autonomy and responsibility in the early stages. His account of these early stages clearly indicates the emphasis placed by the organization on the values of individual achievement: hard work, loyalty, and the all-pervasive concern with the striving for future rewards:

I can only assume that other retail organizations are like this. Once you get inside you seem to be totally committed to a large organization. When you first accept it there is a sort of acceptance ritual – they make you up from stockroom trainee, which really is the lowest of the low, doing all the filthy jobs, and then they finally decide to put you on the floor and make you a floor man. They accept you, and you put a suit on and you get sent to head office where they hand you this company tie and a little certificate. They give you a great propaganda speech telling you what a great place White's is so long as you work hard and it may be tough to start with but in the long run it's worth it. You go back thinking great – I feel really great working for White's.

There was a feeling of total commitment and being a trainee manager they don't pay you enough but they expect a lot from you and they get it by saying 'if you want to get on in this company you've got to work hard now and you will reap the benefits later'. The benefits are fantastic. It was always being pointed out to us that however good you were was completely up to you and that you could earn up to £12,000 a year and things like this.

The manager of the store would say to us consider this as your university degree, whereas another chap might be at university studying you are studying here only being paid for it. It was clever (looking back). The area manager was content with his lot because he was earning a fair whack and he often used to say 'my next-door neighbours are doctors and solicitors and things like that and they might look down on me for being an area manager of a retail group but if I'm earning the same as them I don't give a damn'. I don't know whether it was their own personal policies to put this forward or whether it was group policy.

Despite the clarity with which he could describe the career ladder and the time it normally takes to move from one stage to another Trevor found it difficult to specify the criteria used for promotion:

It was a case of how well you could talk about the various forms which you had to send off. How well you related to other staff. How experienced you looked and sounded. How well you fitted into the White's image.

There were a number of strains in the relationship between Trevor and his parents associated with his upward mobility. These seem to have been brought into focus by the sudden termination of his school career, which greatly disappointed his parents. Whereas for some young people entry into work intensifies such problems, for Trevor it helped him to cope with them:

At the time (of leaving school) my parents were giving me a hell of a lot of pressure to join the Forces (as an officer) and even my father who didn't normally pressurize me into anything had decided that it was the best thing to do. I refused to do it point blank and it was a very bad situation at home. Christopher the accountant was very helpful, I'll always be grateful to him because I used to get very depressed with arguments with my parents. Things were just very bad. It (the job) helped take me out of the way and I started to put some money into the house and it eased the situation a lot but they were still very angry because I wouldn't go into the Forces. I think they are still a bit disappointed but we don't talk about it now.

THE CAREERLESS PERSPECTIVE

Frank

Frank (19) is the oldest of three brothers. His youngest brother is still attending a secondary modern school and his other brother is a factory operative. The family has lived in a terraced house in a traditional working-class area of the city since his parents have been married (21 years). His father is a dustman, and his mother a cleaner. Frank was born when his mother was 17 and his father 19. He attended a secondary-modern school and was placed in the lowest stream there. His account of his school experience emphasized the arbitrary exercise of authority by his teachers and his resentment at the preferential treatment 'good' pupils received:

I was glad to get away from the teachers. If they were wrong and said they were right, they were right. At odd times they had their friends, the good ones – they thought better of some than others. They gave them nice jobs, like marking other boys' books. I think what is good for one is good for another.

He left school as soon as he could but with no educational certificate. All he can remember about the help received in finding a job while at school was that the school organized visits to two factories and that a man from the Youth Employment gave a talk to his class. This latter was not seen as very useful, and the only information he could remember being conveyed was that choice of work:

depends on whether you could stand up all day or sit down all day. If you could sit down you wanted a sitting-down job.

The way in which he describes his choice of job demonstrates the working of informal networks of information and a concern with the 'immediate' characteristics and rewards of careerless work.

A friend got me the job (labourer in a scrap yard). He was the yard foreman. It was an open air job. . . . I couldn't stand working among dust all day (in an indoor job).

He was in his first job for ten months but then got a job through his father as a labourer in the Parks Department.

Although he liked his first job he moved from it in order to gain more security and better money. Again he was attracted by the open-air nature of the work and sees other attractions to it also.

You know when you start and you know when you finish every day. It's an open-air job, and a job for life. He (his boss) doesn't bother you. We hardly ever see him. The foreman's good with you. He has a joke and you can get on with him alright. I gets on with me work-mates alright – one of them showed me how to clean out the hedges. It's just the same as if you're at home – the way you talk and things like that.

His entry into work created no problems for himself or his parents. Unlike the preceding cases his parents left it up to him to find a job:

They left it to me. I've got to be happy in my job. I've got to work there and if I don't like the job it's no good working there and so they told me to pick my own.

By contrast to those following a career Frank's non-work activities were clearly more important to him than his job. He had a large group of friends (eight of whom were waiting for him to finish the interview) with whom he played cards, went out dancing, drinking and the like. He also had an allotment on which he spent a lot of time and kept chickens. Although he is satisfied with his work he is not committed to it:

It's alright, but it could be better. If you ever get married it wouldn't be a very good wage, but it's alright if you are single.

The height of his aspirations in his job is to get a job on the grass-cutting machines.

Main Sources and Further Reading

THE FAMILY

The discussion of the different types of family and their characteristic patterns of socialization draws on a number of empirical studies.

LAWTON, D. *Social Class, Language and Education.* London: Routledge and Kegan Paul, 1968.
The first three chapters and Chapter 5 provide a useful non-technical review of a number of our sources.

KLEIN, M. *Samples from English Cultures*, Vol. 2. London: Routledge and Kegan Paul, 1965.
This is a non-technical, clear and excellent analysis of empirical studies together with a comparative discussion of working-class and middle-class families.

NEWSON, J. & E. *Four Years Old in an Urban Community.* London: Allen and Unwin, 1968.
This Nottingham-based study highlights some of the patterns of socialization which are characteristic of different types of family.

BANKS, O. & FINLAYSON, D. *Success and Failure in the Secondary School.* London: Methuen, 1973.
This provides the most recent study of the relationship between patterns of socialization and school achievement. It also highlights the feed-back between school performance and family relationships.

BOTT, E. *Family and Social Network.* London: Tavistock (2nd Ed.) 1971.
This influential study contrasts working-class and middle-class families and focuses on the significance of broader community relationships for the way in which the families function.

ELIAS, N. & SCOTSON, J. *The Established and the Outsiders.* London: Frank Cass, 1965.
This is another study which demonstrates the influence of com-

munity relationships upon family life. It provides a salutory reminder that the distinction between the 'rough' and 'respectable' elements within the working class does not invariably correspond to the crude index of 'occupational skills' which we have used in this book.

YOUNG, M. & WILLMOTT, P. *The Symmetrical Family: A Study of Work and Leisure in a London Region.* London: Routledge and Kegan Paul, 1973.
This provides the most recent study of family structure, although it tends to overestimate the changes which have occurred, possibly due to the fact that their study was concerned with families living in London.

More detailed studies of middle-class families can be found in:

BELL, C. *Middle Class Families: Social and Geographical Mobility.* London: Routledge and Kegan Paul, 1968.

FOGARTY, M. P. & RAPOPORT, R. & R. *Sex, Career and Family.* London: Allen and Unwin, 1971.

PAHL, J. M. & R. E. *Managers and their Wives.* London: Allen Lane, 1971.

Some representative studies of working-class families are:

YOUNG, M. & WILLMOTT, P. *Family and Kinship in East London.* London: Routledge and Kegan Paul, 1957.

GOLDTHORPE, J. H. *et al. The Affluent Worker in the Class Structure.* London: Cambridge University Press, 1969.

THE EDUCATION SYSTEM

There is a large body of literature about the education system.

BANKS, O. *The Sociology of Education* (3rd Edition). London: Batsford, 1976.
This provides the best general introduction to the field. Chapters 2 and 3 provide a clear and comprehensive summary of much of the literature on the relationship between education and the economy. Chapters 4 and 5 provide a useful summary of the evidence on the relationship between family, social class and school achievement.

CRAFT, M. (ed.). *Family, Class and Education*. London: Longman, 1970.
A useful collection of readings drawn from many of the more detailed sources we consulted.

EGGLESTON, J. (ed.). *Contemporary Research in the Sociology of Education*. London: Methuen, 1974.
Another useful collection of readings.

DOUGLAS, J. W. B. *The Home and the School*. London: MacGibbon & Kee, 1964.
An early but useful discussion of the relationship between home and school and the effects of streaming in the state school system.

SWIFT, B. 'Job Orientation and the Transition from School to Work: a Longitudinal Study'. *British Journal of Guidance and Counselling*, Vol. 1, No. 1, 1973.
An important article demonstrating the impact of school experience on the job prospects of young people. The weak effect which streaming in the secondary modern school had on the career prospects of the young workers reported here may well be due to the characteristics of the London labour market in which her sample was employed.

TAYLOR, G. & AYRES, N. *Born and Bred Unequal*. London: Longman, 1970.
A thorough documentation of the regional variations in the provision of education.

Useful accounts of the different types of school and their impact on the children attending them can be found in the following studies:

HARGREAVES, D. H. *Social Relations in a Secondary School*. London: Routledge and Kegan Paul, 1967.

LACEY, C. *Hightown Grammar*. Manchester University Press, 1970.

KING, R. *Values and Involvement in a Grammar School*. London: Routledge and Kegan Paul, 1969.

FORD, J. *Social Class and the Comprehensive School*. London: Routledge and Kegan Paul, 1969.

GUTHRIE, R. 'Neighbourhood School' in P. Barker (ed.), *One for Sorrow Two for Joy: Ten Years of New Society*. London: Allen and Unwin, 1972, pp. 324–36.

PARTRIDGE, J. *Life in a Secondary Modern School*. Harmondsworth, Middx.: Penguin, 1970.

EGGLESTON, J. 'Research and the Comprehensives', *Times Educational Supplement*, 24 January 1975, pp. 22–3.

Provides a clear and useful examination of the findings of recent research on the impact of comprehensive schools, and suggests that they have had little effect on the grammar schools.

THE TRANSITION FROM SCHOOL TO WORK

The empirical material on which the analysis of the transition from school to work is based is drawn from a number of sources in addition to the Leicester project referred to earlier. The studies listed below are all based on survey research. The major problem in using survey research is that in the absence of any agreed framework of analysis it is frequently difficult to make valid comparison of the results.

CARTER, M. P. *Home, School and Work*. London: Pergamon Press, 1962.

A study of 100 boys and 100 girls who left schools in Sheffield in 1959.

MAIZELS, E. J. *Adolescent Needs and the Transition from School to Work*. London: Athlone Press, 1970.

A useful study of over 300 boys and girls in Willesden, Middlesex and of 75 firms covering the main phases involved in the transition from school to work.

SCHOOLS COUNCIL ENQUIRY I. *Young School Leavers*. London: HMSO Government Social Survey, 1968.

Based on a large national sample of young people, parents and teachers, and provides a useful factual and statistical picture of England and Wales.

OFFICE OF POPULATION CENSUS AND SURVEYS. *Looking Forward to Work,* and *Fifth Form Girls: Their Hopes for the Future*. London: HMSO, 1974 and 1975.

Extensive survey reports of young people still at school and their hopes and orientations to work. These became available after the main body of the book was written and so we have been unable to incorporate their findings systematically into our discussion. The findings of these reports add considerable support to our argument.

HALE, S. *Idle Hill: Prospect for Young Workers in a Rural Area*. London: National Council for Social Services, 1971.

Presents interesting data on the transition from school to work for a rural sample of both sexes in Herefordshire.

CARTER, M. P. *Into Work*. Harmondsworth, Middx.: Penguin, 1969.

A broadly based factual discussion of the transition from school to work.

WILLIAMS, W. M. (ed.). *Occupational Choice*. London: Allen & Unwin, 1974.

BUTLER, M. A. *Occupational Choice*. London: HMSO, 1968.

These two publications between them adequately cover the various theories which have been put forward to explain occupational choice. As we have indicated, we do not feel that such theories have been very useful.

BRANNEN, P. (ed.). *Entering the World of Work: some sociological perspectives*. Department of Employment, London, HMSO, 1975.

A recent and useful collection of papers which provide a detailed discussion of some of the issues we have raised above.

THE OCCUPATIONAL STRUCTURE

The discussion of the occupational structure is primarily based on the analysis of census returns for a number of years.

ROUTH, G. *Occupation and Pay in Great Britain 1906–1960*. London: Cambridge University Press, 1965.

Provides a thorough analysis of the material, although the categories used are slightly different from those we use in Chapter 2.

GLASS, D. V. (ed.). *Social Mobility in Britain*. London: Routledge and Kegan Paul, 1954.

Provides the most comprehensive study of social mobility presently available. There is currently a study of social mobility being conducted at Oxford which will supersede this volume.

HALL, R. H. *Occupations and the Social Structure*. Englewood Cliffs, New Jersey: Prentice Hall, 1969.

Provides an excellent, clear and readable account of the occupational structure of modern industrial society. The major drawback to it is that most of the empirical material referred to deals with the USA. However, we feel that in its broad outlines the picture drawn is applicable to present British society.

ALLSOP, K. *A New Deal for Young Workers*. London: Zenith, 1966.

Contains a useful discussion of the different types of occupations open to young people and clearly indicates the differences in opportunities available to young men and young women.

DEPARTMENT OF EMPLOYMENT. *Unqualified, Untrained and Unemployed*. Report of a Working Party set up by the National Youth Employment Council. London: HMSO, 1974.

A very useful and up-to-date account of the job opportunities available to school leavers, and the effects of regional variations upon them. It is primarily concerned with the careerless and the problems they experience.

FRASER, R. (ed.). *Work* and *Work 2*. Harmondsworth, Middx.: Penguin, 1968, 1969.
These provide vivid and readable personal accounts of work, although these are not necessarily representative of all the people employed in these occupations.

WEIR, D. (ed.). *Men and Work in Modern Britain*. London: Fontana, 1973.
This is a rather uneven collection of readings about work situations and work experiences. Despite its title it covers both male and female occupations. Some of the readings are very useful.

SCEAR, N., ROBERTS, V. & BROCK, J. *A Career for Women in Industry*. London: Oliver and Boyd, 1964.
Documents the difficulties women face in making a career at work, and their attitude towards industrial careers.

OAKLEY, A. *The Sociology of Housework*. Bath: Martin Robertson, 1974.
Provides a thorough and stimulating discussion of women and work which is placed in the general context of the socialization of women in the family and their general position in society.

There have been a number of studies of different occupations. Representative British studies are listed below.

SOFER, C. *Men in Mid-Career: A Study of British Managers and Technical Specialists*. London: Cambridge University Press, 1970.
An excellent study of 'middle level' executives and specialists working in industrial organizations, and the ways in which their work experiences affected their self-conceptions.

LOCKWOOD, D. *The Black-coated Worker: A Study in Class Consciousness*. London: Allen and Unwin, 1958.
This study of clerical workers, while dated, provides one of the best sociological analyses of an occupational group.

GOLDTHORPE, J. H. *et al.* *The Affluent Workers: Industrial Attitudes and Behaviour*. London: Cambridge University Press, 1969.
A fairly thorough sociological analysis of industrial workers.

BEYNON, H. *Working for Ford*. London: Allan Lane, 1973.
A lively account of how assembly line work is experienced.

180

WEDDERBURN, D. & CROMPTON, R. *Workers' Attitudes and Technology*. London: Cambridge University Press, 1972.
A case study of some of the work-based determinants of workers' perspectives. This contains a useful discussion of the ways in which the autonomy provided by skilled work provides an important basis for the development of the workers' views of themselves and the world. This is contrasted to the work situation of the semi-skilled.

Very little work has been done focusing directly upon the work experiences of young people.

BROWN, R. 'The attitudes to work, expectations and social perspectives of shipbuilding apprentices', in T. Leggatt (ed.), *Sociological Theory and Survey Research: Institutional Change and Social Policy in Great Britain*. London: Sage, 1975.
This provides a valuable account of the perspectives of shipbuilding apprentices.
VENABLES, E. *The Young Worker at College. A Study of a Local Tech*. Faber and Faber: London, 1967.
VENABLES, E. *Apprentices Out of Their Time: A Follow-up Study*. London: Faber and Faber, 1974.
This study is focused on the part played by the college in the lives of apprentices and also provides useful data on the distinctiveness of their perspectives.

PROBLEMS OF ADJUSTMENT TO WORK

The evidence on which our discussion of the severe problems of adjustment to work is based is largely drawn from work carried out on the Leicester project and on the work of students in the Department of Sociology at Leicester University in recent years. We suggest that one of the reasons for the poverty of data in this area is the lack of a general framework within which such problems can be located. The more indirect evidence, which points to the problems we have discussed, is mainly found in reports of work carried out among 'unattached' youth. Most of these studies were conducted in areas and times of full employment.

MORSE, M. *The Unattached*. Harmondsworth, Middlesex: Pelican Books, 1965.
A report of a 3-year project carried out by the National Associa-

tion of Youth Clubs into those middle-class young people they fail to attract, many of which were encountering 'severe' problems of adjustment to work.

PHILLIPS, D. 'Young and Unemployed in a Northern City' in D. Weir (ed.) *Men and Work in Modern Britain,* op. cit.
This contains a useful description of 'chronic job changers' and their problems.

At Odds. Report of the Working Party of the National Youth Employment Council. London: HMSO, 1970.
A somewhat impressionistic account of those young people who experience difficulties in holding down jobs.

Unemployment and Homelessness. A Report. Community Relations Commission. Home Office. London: HMSO, 1974.
This report highlights the problems among West Indian youths.

The Problems of Coloured School Leavers. Report of the Select Committee on Race Relations and Immigration. London: HMSO, 1969.

ALLEN, S. & SMITH, C. 'Race and Ethnicity in Class Formation: A Comparison of Asian and West Indian Workers', in F. Parkin (ed.) *The Social Analysis of Class Structure.* London: Tavistock, 1974.
A short but useful discussion of the main differences between some immigrant groups.

SMITH C. S., FARRANT, M. R. & MARCHANT, H. J. *The Wincroft Youth Project: a social work programme in a slum area,* London, Tavistock, 1972.
A thorough and sophisticated study of unattached working-class youths in Manchester and their relationships with social workers.

JONES, P., SMITH, G. & PULHAM, K. *All Their Future: A Study of the problems of a group of school leavers in a disadvantaged area of Liverpool.*
Department of Social and Administrative Studies, Oxford University, 1975.
This report appeared after the book was written and adds further confirmation to many aspects of our analysis of the problem of the careerless.

HELPING AGENCIES

ROBERTS, K. *From School to Work.* A Study of the Youth Employment Service. Newton Abbot: David and Charles, 1972.
This provides a comprehensive analysis of the structure and function of the Youth Employment Service.

Careers Education in Secondary Schools. Education Survey 18, Department of Education and Science. London: HMSO.
This is useful for the factual information it contains.

The following journals provide important sources of information:

Careers Quarterly. The Journal of the Institute of Careers Officers.
Youth in Society. The Journal of the National Youth Bureau.
Careers Bulletin. Department of Employment.
The Careers and Guidance Teacher. The Journal of the National Association of Careers and Guidance Teachers.
Education and Training (formerly Technical Education).
The Vocational Aspects of Education.
The Training Officer. The Journal of the Institution of Training Officers.
Industrial Society (formerly Industrial Welfare).

CONCEPTUALIZATION

The theoretical perspective which we have adopted in this book draws on a number of sources within the fields of Sociology and Social Psychology. In addition to the work of Elias mentioned earlier, the following is a list of the most influential sources.

BECKER, H. S. 'Notes on the concept of commitment', *American Journal of Sociology* (1960) 66: pp. 32–40.
The basis of our ideas about the ways in which young people become progressively 'locked into' certain types of occupation as a result of their life experiences.
BERNSTEIN, B. (ed.). *Class, Codes and Control*, Vols. 1 and 2. London: Routledge and Kegan Paul, 1971 and 1973.
Bernstein provided an important source for our thinking about the general nature of the relationships between work, family and school, although Bernstein and his colleagues mainly restrict their empirical attention to patterns of language use and social control within families.
Volume 1 is a collection of theoretical papers of which the most useful are those contained in Part III; Volume 2 is mainly a collection of papers reporting on the research findings of Bernstein and his colleagues.
STRAUSS, A. L. *Mirrors and Masks*. Glencoe, Ill.: Free Press, 1959; and 'Some Neglected Properties of Status Passage', in H. S.

Becker *et al.*, *Institutions and the Person*. Chicago: Aldine Press, 1968.
Provided the basis for the way in which we view the processual character of social life, and the importance of taking this fully into account.

TURNER, R. 'Role-Taking: Process versus Conformity', in A. M. Rose (ed.), *Human Behaviour and Social Processes*. London: Routledge and Kegan Paul, 1962, pp. 20–40.
Was important in helping us think about the types of relationships with others which people enter into, and the consequences of these.

GIDDENS, A. *The Class Structure of the Advanced Societies*. London: Hutchinson University Library, 1973.
A good, but high level, discussion of social class in modern industrial societies. Giddens addresses many of the points we make in this book, but at a high level of generality. The book is useful as it locates our discussion in the broader debate about the character of industrial societies.

Three academic publications by us spell out the linkages between these (and other) influences.

ASHTON, D. N. 'Careers and commitment: The movement from school to work', in David Field (ed.), *Social Psychology for Sociologists*. London: T. Nelson and Sons, 1974, pp. 171–86.
This, together with Ashton 'The transition from school to work', op. cit., provides the initial conceptualization upon which the present book is based.

FIELD, D. 'Introduction' to *Social Psychology for Sociologists,* op. cit.
This spells out the general 'model of man' which informs this book.

ASHTON, D. N. & FIELD, D. 'The transition from school to work', in S. J. Eggleston (ed.), *Paedogogica Europaea: A yearbook of educational research,* 1975, 10.
This presents aspects of our conceptualization of social class in more detail.

Index

Compiled by Gordon Robinson